Medical Terminology Study Guide

The Complete Study Guide to Easily Understand, Pronounce and Memorize Medical Terms

Exam Master

Introduction
Purpose of the Guide

The "Medical Terminology Study Guide" is designed to unravel the complexities of medical terminology for a diverse audience, including students, healthcare professionals, and anyone interested in the medical field. The primary goal of this guide is to provide a thorough resource that not only introduces fundamental aspects of medical vocabulary but also improves users' abilities to understand, pronounce, and memorize these terms efficiently.

Medical terminology is the cornerstone of effective communication within healthcare environments. Mastery of this language is crucial for conveying precise and clear information, which is integral to diagnosing, treating, and managing patients. Accuracy in medical communication can dramatically influence patient outcomes, making the understanding of these terms vital for healthcare professionals.

This guide aims to equip learners with the necessary skills to excel in their educational pursuits and professional careers. It caters to a wide range of users, from students embarking on their medical journey to seasoned practitioners aiming to enhance their knowledge base. Even individuals with a burgeoning interest in medical terms will find this guide invaluable. Through carefully structured content, practical exercises, and visual aids, this guide facilitates an engaging and comprehensive learning experience.

Enhancing Communication in Healthcare

Effective communication is pivotal in healthcare settings. Misunderstandings can lead to errors in patient care, affecting the quality of treatments and outcomes. This guide addresses these challenges by providing clear explanations, examples, and practice scenarios that help solidify the use of medical terminology in a variety of clinical interactions and documentation processes.

Supporting Professional Development

The guide supports professional development by enhancing the reader's vocabulary and understanding of medical terms. This is particularly beneficial in a professional's ability to engage with peers, partake in research, and understand complex medical literature. As professionals advance in their careers, a deep understanding of medical terminology facilitates specialization, allowing them to delve deeper into specific areas such as oncology, pediatrics, or cardiology.

Facilitating Academic Success

For students, this guide serves as an essential tool for academic success. Medical courses heavily rely on terminology, and understanding these terms is often a prerequisite for advanced studies and clinical practices. The guide's structured approach helps students build a solid foundation of medical language, crucial for passing exams and participating in clinical discussions.

Promoting Continuous Learning

The medical field is ever-evolving with new technologies, treatments, and discoveries continually emerging. This guide encourages continuous learning by providing up-to-date information and resources. It serves as a springboard for further exploration and understanding of advanced topics, ensuring that learners remain knowledgeable and competent in a fast-paced and changing industry.

Aiding Global Collaboration

The standardization of medical terminology makes it a universal language in global health. This guide facilitates international collaboration by helping users from different geographical backgrounds communicate more effectively. This is especially important in global health initiatives, research studies, and epidemiological tracking, where clear and precise communication is essential.

Improving Patient Care and Safety

One of the guide's fundamental aims is to improve patient care and safety. By understanding medical terminology, healthcare professionals can accurately document patient interactions, understand patient needs, and coordinate care effectively. This leads to better patient management, fewer errors, and improved health outcomes.

Enhancing Telemedicine

As telemedicine becomes more prevalent, the need for clear communication becomes even more critical. This guide helps healthcare professionals engage in telehealth interactions with confidence, ensuring they can provide high-quality care remotely. This is particularly important in rural or underserved areas where access to healthcare professionals is limited.

Streamlining Healthcare Administration

Administrators and other non-medical staff also benefit from understanding medical terminology. This guide helps those involved in the administrative aspects of healthcare, such as billing and coding, to perform their duties more efficiently and accurately. This not only improves workflow but also ensures compliance with healthcare regulations and insurance requirements.

Supporting Research and Innovation

Researchers in the medical field will find this guide helpful in their work, whether they are conducting clinical trials, writing research papers, or developing new medical technologies. A thorough understanding of medical terminology is essential for analyzing data, sharing findings, and collaborating with other experts in the field.

Ultimately, this guide is more than just a textbook; it is a comprehensive tool designed to empower its readers. By demystifying medical terminology, it aims to enhance communication, support professional and academic growth, promote safety, and foster ongoing learning within the medical community. The "Medical Terminology Study Guide" is an indispensable resource for anyone looking to deepen their understanding of this critical aspect of healthcare.

How to Use This Guide

To get the most out of this study guide on medical terminology, adopting certain study habits and strategies is essential. Here's how you can optimize your learning experience:

Regular Study Sessions

Setting a Schedule: Establishing a dedicated study schedule is crucial. Allocate specific times each day for studying medical terminology to help form a consistent study habit that facilitates easier learning and better retention of information.

Creating a Study Environment: Choose a quiet and comfortable study area free from distractions. A well-organized environment conducive to learning can significantly enhance your focus and productivity.

Duration of Study Sessions: It's important to determine the length of your study sessions. Typically, sessions of 25-50 minutes are effective, followed by short breaks. This technique, often referred to as the Pomodoro Technique, helps maintain concentration and stamina over time.

Daily Goals: Set clear, achievable goals for each session, such as mastering a specific number of terms or thoroughly understanding certain concepts. Such goals keep you motivated and give a sense of accomplishment.

Consistency: Consistency is key in any learning endeavor. Try to study at the same time each day to establish a routine that becomes a natural part of your daily life, enhancing the overall learning experience.

Active Learning

Engagement with Materials: Active engagement means not just reading the material but interacting with it. Utilize the practice questions and other interactive elements in the guide to apply what you have learned.

Discussion Groups: Join or form study groups where you can discuss and reinforce learning. Explaining terms to others is a powerful way to deepen your own understanding.

Teaching Others: Try to teach the concepts you learn to someone else. Teaching is a highly effective learning technique as it forces you to process and clarify the information.

Practical Application: Whenever possible, apply the medical terms in practical scenarios, such as case studies or simulations. This application helps in cementing the information in your memory.

Feedback: Seek feedback on your understanding from peers or instructors. Feedback is crucial as it helps identify areas where more focus is needed and reinforces areas where you are strong.

Utilize Visual Aids

Diagrams and Charts: Make extensive use of diagrams, charts, and other visual aids provided in the guide. Visual learning aids are incredibly effective for subjects like medical terminology where visualizing the information can lead to better retention.

Creating Your Own Visuals: Apart from using the provided visuals, try creating your own diagrams or charts based on your notes. This activity enhances understanding and memory by engaging multiple senses.

Mnemonics: Develop mnemonics or memory aids that help you remember complex terms. Visual mnemonics are particularly useful in memorizing prefixes, suffixes, and root words.

Flashcards: Utilize flashcards with terms on one side and definitions or diagrams on the other. These are excellent for quick revision and self-testing.

Mind Maps: Create mind maps to visualize the connections between different medical terms, especially when studying body systems or related pathological conditions.

Repetition

Scheduled Review Sessions: Incorporate regular review sessions into your study routine. Revisiting the material at spaced intervals is a proven method to improve memory retention.

Use of Flashcards: Regularly use flashcards to drill the terms. This repetitive practice is crucial for transferring knowledge from short-term to long-term memory.

Consolidation: At the end of each study session, spend a few minutes summarizing what you've learned. This repetition of information helps consolidate the memory and improves recall.

Incremental Addition: As you progress through the guide, continually add new terms to your revision sessions without neglecting older information, ensuring a comprehensive understanding and retention.

Testing Frequency: Increase the frequency of quizzes and tests. Regular testing not only assesses your knowledge but also reinforces learning through repetition.

Incremental Learning

Foundational to Advanced: Start with the foundational concepts of medical terminology before progressing to more specialized terms. This builds a solid base that makes understanding complex concepts easier.

Structured Learning Path: Follow the structured path provided in the guide. Each chapter is designed to naturally lead into the next, gradually increasing in complexity.

Layered Learning: Revisit basic concepts periodically even as you move into more advanced topics. This layering of information helps in creating a deeper understanding and retention.

Goal Setting: Set progressive learning goals that reflect your advancement through the guide. For example, begin with learning basic word roots before moving on to full terms and their applications.

Pace Yourself: Adjust your learning pace based on your understanding of the material. If a particular section is challenging, take extra time to master it before moving on.

By incorporating these strategies into your study habits, you can maximize the effectiveness of this guide and ensure a deep and lasting understanding of medical terminology.

Overview of Medical Terminology

Medical terminology is like the building blocks of a language, composed of word roots, prefixes, and suffixes that are primarily derived from Greek and Latin. This structured approach not only systematizes medical communication but also forms the foundation of a vast majority of medical terms. Each component plays a critical role in forming the precise terms used across various aspects of healthcare.

Word Roots

Core Meaning: Word roots are typically derived from Greek or Latin and usually indicate the part of the body or the primary concept of the term. Understanding the root of a term can often give clues about its general meaning even before other elements are added.

Examples and Usage: For instance, the root "cardio-" refers to the heart, "neuro-" pertains to the nervous system, and "dermat-" relates to the skin. Recognizing these roots can help in quickly understanding the focus of medical discussions or documents.

Combination Flexibility: Roots can be combined with other roots to form more complex terms that describe more specific conditions or anatomical structures, like "cardiopulmonary" (heart and lungs) or "neurobiology" (study of the biology of the nervous system).

Structural Understanding: Gaining familiarity with various roots enhances one's ability to decipher medical terms that may not be explicitly taught but encountered in professional settings.

Practical Application: Learning word roots is crucial for medical students and professionals who need to quickly grasp the essence of medical conditions or treatments during studies or in clinical settings.

Prefixes

Modification of Meaning: Prefixes are added to the beginning of word roots to modify their meanings by providing additional details about location, time, nature, or quantity.

Common Prefixes: Examples include "hypo-" meaning under or below normal, "hyper-" meaning over or excessive, and "peri-" meaning around. These prefixes can significantly alter the meaning of the terms they precede, such as turning "thermal" (pertaining to heat) into "hypothermal" (below normal temperature).

Enhancing Precision: By modifying the root term, prefixes help in describing more precisely the nature of a condition or procedure, which is essential for accurate diagnosis and treatment.

Contextual Clarity: Prefixes offer clarity in medical contexts by helping specify medical terms, especially when similar conditions or procedures affect different parts of the body or occur under different circumstances.

Learning Strategy: Memorizing common prefixes can accelerate the learning process and improve the understanding of medical literature, enhancing communication skills in a clinical context.

Suffixes

Describing Conditions or Processes: Suffixes are attached to the end of word roots and often describe the condition, disease process, or procedure. They play a key role in tailoring the medical term to a specific condition or action.

Examples and Functions: For example, "-itis" denotes inflammation, thus "arthritis" means inflammation of the joints. "-ectomy" means the removal of, so "appendectomy" refers to the surgical removal of the appendix.

Diagnostic and Procedural Implications: Understanding suffixes is particularly important for professionals involved in diagnostics and procedural medical roles, as it aids in precisely identifying the nature of the medical intervention.

Systematic Learning: Learning suffixes helps in systematically building a medical vocabulary that supports effective and efficient communication in healthcare settings.

Integration in Practice: Regular use and exposure to these suffixes in practical scenarios, such as case studies or clinical procedures, reinforce their meanings and applications, making them second nature to medical professionals.

Understanding and mastering these components of medical terminology are fundamental to navigating the medical field with confidence and accuracy. This knowledge not only supports medical communication but also enhances comprehension and application of medical concepts in real-world healthcare scenarios.

In conclusion, the importance of understanding medical terminology cannot be overstated, as it is fundamental to the effective communication and operation within any healthcare environment. This guide has been designed not only to introduce medical terms but also to provide you with the tools and strategies to master this crucial language. By dedicating yourself to regular study sessions, engaging actively with the material, and utilizing visual aids, you can build a robust foundation that will support your professional or academic pursuits in the medical field.

Furthermore, the structured approach to learning that includes active engagement and incremental learning will facilitate the absorption and retention of medical terminology. Whether you are a student, a practicing professional, or simply an interested individual, adopting these strategies will enhance your ability to navigate through complex medical dialogues and documentation with confidence and precision.

The overview of word roots, prefixes, and suffixes provided in this guide serves as a cornerstone for delving deeper into the language of medicine. By understanding these basic elements, you are better equipped to decode and comprehend complex medical terms, which will invariably enrich your understanding of medical texts, improve communication with colleagues and patients, and elevate your academic and professional performance.

Introduction

As you continue to explore and utilize this guide, remember that mastering medical terminology is a progressive journey that requires patience, practice, and perseverance. The consistent application of the learning strategies outlined here will not only deepen your knowledge but also enhance your ability to apply this knowledge in practical settings.

Finally, this guide is intended to be a dynamic tool in your educational toolkit. It is my hope that it will inspire continued learning and curiosity about the medical world, fostering a lifelong commitment to excellence in whatever healthcare arena you choose to pursue. Remember, each term mastered is a step closer to a greater understanding and more effective participation in the world of medicine.

Chapter 1
Basics of Medical Language

Understanding the foundation of medical terminology is pivotal for anyone embarking on a career in healthcare. This foundational knowledge comprises word roots, prefixes, suffixes, and combining forms—each serving as a critical building block in the intricate language of medicine. Here's a deeper look at why mastery of these elements is essential:

1. **Basis for Medical Language**: Medical terminology operates almost as a sub-language within English, heavily borrowing from ancient Greek and Latin. These languages were chosen due to their precise vocabularies, which are crucial for the exacting nature of science and medicine. Word roots, often derived from these languages, provide the base meaning of terms used to describe body parts, functions, diseases, and procedures. Understanding these roots allows medical professionals to break down complex terms into understandable components.

2. **Enhancing Communication**: In healthcare, effective communication can literally be a matter of life and death. Medical professionals use terminology as a shorthand for complex procedures and diagnoses, ensuring clarity and precision in communication. For instance, a well-understood term among professionals can convey a wealth of information that might otherwise require lengthy explanations. Mastery of prefixes, suffixes, and combining forms allows healthcare workers to modify and adapt terms to convey exact meanings, which improves the efficiency and accuracy of medical communication.

3. **Facilitating Learning and Memory**: The systematic structure of medical terms, thanks to these basic components, helps students and professionals not only learn but also retain medical vocabulary more effectively. By understanding the meaning of a prefix or a suffix, one can deduce the meaning of new terms encountered in practice or study. This structured approach to vocabulary building can significantly ease the learning curve for students in medical education and professionals keeping up with new terminology in their fields.

4. **Enabling Quick Adaptation to New Concepts**: The medical field is continually evolving with new discoveries and technologies. Existing terms often need to be adapted or new terms created to describe these advancements. A solid grasp of the basic components of medical terminology makes it easier to understand and assimilate these new concepts quickly. For example, when a new disease is discovered, understanding the components of its name can help healthcare professionals quickly grasp its nature, affected body parts, and potential treatments based on the name alone.

5. **Cross-disciplinary Understanding**: Medical terminology is not only used by doctors and nurses but also by many other professionals in the healthcare industry, such as pharmacists, biomedical scientists, and radiologists. A common understanding of medical terminology helps facilitate interdisciplinary collaboration and enhances the overall efficiency of healthcare delivery. This shared vocabulary allows for smoother transitions between different departments and specialties, enabling more cohesive and integrated patient care.

In essence, the foundational knowledge of word roots, prefixes, suffixes, and combining forms in medical terminology is more than just academic requirement—it's a critical tool that empowers professionals across the healthcare spectrum to communicate effectively, learn continuously, and deliver high-quality care.

Word Roots

Word roots are the foundational elements of medical terminology, acting as the cornerstone upon which most medical terms are built. They generally represent a body part or a fundamental concept within the medical field, providing essential clues about the meanings of complex terms.

Significance of Word Roots

Word roots are integral for anyone studying or working in the healthcare sector because they form the base of the language used to describe nearly every aspect of the body and its conditions. By understanding these roots, healthcare professionals can dissect complicated medical terms and grasp their meanings, aiding in diagnosis, treatment, and communication.

Function in Medical Terms

Word roots serve as the primary lexicon in medical terminology to which prefixes and suffixes are added to modify meanings. This modification allows medical terms to be precisely tailored to describe specific conditions, anatomical structures, or procedures. For instance, the root "cardi-" implies a relation to the heart. When combined with "-ology," which pertains to the study of, the resulting term "cardiology" clearly defines the field concerned with heart-related studies.

Detailed Examples of Word Roots

1. **Gastro-**: This root is derived from the Greek word "gastēr," meaning stomach. In medical terminology, "gastro-" is used to denote terms related to the stomach. An example is "gastroenterology," the study of the stomach and intestines' structure, function, and disorders.
2. **Hemat-**: Originating from the Greek word "haima" meaning blood, "hemat-" is used in terms related to blood. For example, "hematology" focuses on the study of blood, blood-forming organs, and blood diseases.
3. **Neuro-**: This root comes from the Greek word "neuron," meaning nerve. It is used in terms related to the nerves and the nervous system. "Neurology," therefore, is the branch of medicine dealing with disorders of the nervous system.

Practical Applications in Medical Discussions

Understanding word roots is crucial for medical professionals as it helps specify the focus of medical discussions or diagnoses. For example:

- **Cardi-**: Beyond "cardiology," this root appears in terms like "cardiotoxicity," which refers to the quality of being toxic to the heart, specifically in reference to drugs or other substances.

Medical Terminology Study Guide

- **Dermat-**: Found in terms such as "dermatitis," which refers to inflammation of the skin, illustrating how roots can quickly convey significant clinical information.
- **Nephro-**: Associated with the kidneys, as seen in "nephrology," the study of kidney diseases, and "nephrolithiasis," which refers to the presence of kidney stones.
- **Hepato-**: Related to the liver. Terms include "hepatology," the branch of medicine concerning liver diseases, and "hepatotoxicity," indicating liver damage caused by chemicals.
- **Pulmo-**: Pertains to the lungs. "Pulmonology" deals with respiratory tract diseases, and "pulmonary embolism" describes a blockage in the lungs' blood supply.
- **Gyneco-**: Concerns women's health, particularly the reproductive system. "Gynecology" is the field focused on female reproductive health, and "gynecologist" is a specialist in this area.
- **Onc-**: Relates to tumors or cancer. "Oncology" is the study and treatment of tumors, with "oncologist" being a specialist who treats cancer.
- **Oto-**: Involves the ears. "Otology" is the medical study of the ear and its diseases. "Otitis" refers to ear inflammation, often seen in otitis externa.
- **Neuro-**: Beyond "neurology," the term "neuropathy" is used for conditions involving nerve damage or dysfunction, often leading to numbness or pain.
- **Ortho-**: Means straight or correct. "Orthopedics" focuses on correcting bone and muscle deformities. "Orthopedic surgery" involves the surgical treatment of the skeletal system.
- **Endo-**: Indicates internal or within. "Endocrinology" examines the endocrine glands and their hormones, while "endoscope" is used for internal examinations.

- **Psycho-**: Related to the mind. "Psychology" explores mental processes and behaviors, and "psychosis" describes a severe mental disorder affecting reality perception.

These examples help illustrate the breadth of medical terminology and its crucial role in various medical specialties, enhancing both communication and understanding within the healthcare community.

Expanding Vocabulary with Word Roots

Learning medical terminology through word roots can significantly expand one's medical vocabulary. Each root can lead to dozens of terms when combined with different prefixes and suffixes. For example:

- **Osteo-** (bone): When combined with different suffixes, it can lead to "osteoporosis" (a condition characterized by decreased bone density and strength) or "osteopathy" (a branch of medicine that emphasizes the treatment of medical disorders through the manipulation and massage of the bones, joints, and muscles).
- **Arthro- (joint)**: Used in terms such as "arthritis" (inflammation of a joint) and "arthroscopy" (a procedure for diagnosing and treating joint problems).
- **Myo- (muscle)**: Found in "myopathy" (a disease of muscle tissue) and "myoplasty" (surgical repair of a muscle).
- **Hemo- (blood)**: Appears in "hemoglobin" (the protein in red blood cells that carries oxygen) and "hemostasis" (the stopping of a flow of blood).

Medical Terminology Study Guide

- **Glyco- (sugar)**: Used in "glycogen" (a form of sugar stored in the body) and "hypoglycemia" (abnormally low blood sugar levels).
- **Nephro- (kidney)**: As mentioned, used in "nephrectomy" (surgical removal of a kidney) and "nephritis" (inflammation of the kidneys).
- **Neuro- (nerve)**: In addition to "neurology," terms like "neuroma" (a growth or tumor of nerve tissue) and "neurotoxic" (harmful to the nervous system).
- **Dermato- (skin)**: Used in "dermatology" (the study of skin and its diseases) and "dermatoplasty" (surgical repair of the skin).
- **Hepato- (liver)**: Besides "hepatology," includes "hepatitis" (inflammation of the liver) and "hepatectomy" (surgical removal of part of the liver).
- **Pneumo- (lung)**: Found in "pneumonia" (an infection in the lungs) and "pneumonectomy" (surgical removal of a lung or part of a lung).
- **Gastro- (stomach)**: Used in "gastroenteritis" (inflammation of the stomach and intestines) and "gastrectomy" (surgical removal of part or all of the stomach).
- **Angio- (vessel)**: Appears in "angiography" (an imaging test of the blood vessels) and "angiosclerosis" (hardening of the blood vessels).
- **Oto- (ear)**: Used in "otitis" (as previously mentioned, inflammation of the ear) and "otoplasty" (surgical repair of the ear).
- **Cardio- (heart)**: Found in "cardiomegaly" (enlargement of the heart) and "cardiomyopathy" (disease of the heart muscle).
- **Sclero- (hard)**: Used in "sclerosis" (hardening of tissue, especially from excessive growth of fibrous tissue) and "scleroderma" (a group of autoimmune diseases that may

result in changes to the skin, blood vessels, muscles, and internal organs).

- **Psycho- (mind)**: Besides "psychology," includes "psychopathy" (a personality disorder characterized by persistent antisocial behavior, impaired empathy and remorse, and bold, disinhibited, and egotistical traits) and "psychosomatic" (pertaining to a physical illness or other condition caused or aggravated by a mental factor such as internal conflict or stress).

By mastering these word roots, students and professionals alike enhance their ability to communicate effectively within the medical community, ensuring precise and clear conveyance of information. This depth of understanding not only aids in their current medical practices but also prepares them for continuous learning, as medical terminology evolves with advances in medical science.

Prefixes

Prefixes in medical terminology are essential elements that precede word roots to modify or refine their meanings. They play a critical role by providing additional context that can denote time, location, quantity, or condition, thus altering the interpretation of the terms they precede. This added layer of specificity is crucial in the medical field where precise communication can greatly influence clinical outcomes.

Definition and Function

A prefix is a syllable placed at the beginning of a word to adjust or enhance its meaning. In medical terminology, prefixes help to specify medical instructions and descriptions, making them more exact. For example:

- **"Pre-"** denotes something occurring before a certain point in time, as in "prenatal," which refers to the period before birth.

Medical Terminology Study Guide

- **"Epi-"** indicates upon or above; "epidermis" is the outermost layer of the skin.
- **"A-" or "An-"** generally signifies absence or lack; "anemia" describes a lack of a normal number of red blood cells.
- **"Post-"** indicates after or following; "postoperative" refers to the period after a surgical operation.
- **"Peri-"** means around; "pericardium" is the membrane enclosing the heart.
- **"Anti-"** denotes against or opposed to; "antibiotic" refers to a substance used to kill or inhibit the growth of bacteria.
- **"Intra-"** signifies within or inside; "intravenous" means within or administered through a vein.
- **"Inter-"** indicates between; "intercellular" refers to something occurring between the cells.
- **"Trans-"** denotes across, through, or beyond; "transdermal" describes administration through the skin.
- **"Sub-"** indicates under, below, or less; "subnormal" refers to something below what is considered normal.
- **"Poly-"** means many; "polydipsia" refers to excessive thirst, a condition seen frequently in diabetes.
- **"Neo-"** signifies new; "neonatal" refers to the newborn period, the first few weeks after birth.
- **"Macro-"** indicates large or long; "macromolecule" refers to a molecule of a large size, such as proteins or nucleic acids.
- **"Micro-"** means small; "microscope" is an instrument used to view small objects that cannot be seen with the naked eye.
- **"Exo-"** denotes outside or external; "exoskeleton" refers to a rigid external covering for the body in some invertebrates.

. . .

These prefixes are fundamental to forming precise and descriptive medical terms, aiding healthcare professionals in their daily communications and diagnoses.

Usage in Medical Terms

Prefixes are extensively used across medical terminology to fine-tune and elaborate on the meanings of terms, often essential for the correct diagnosis, treatment, and communication within healthcare settings. For instance:

- **"Hyperglycemia"**: Here, "hyper-" signifies an excess or high level, referring to an unusually high concentration of glucose in the blood.
- **"Hypotension"**: In this term, "hypo-" indicates below normal, thus describing lower than normal blood pressure.
- **"Hypoglycemia"**: "Hypo-" indicates below normal levels, describing unusually low blood glucose levels.
- **"Hypertrophy"**: "Hyper-" signifies excessive or over, referring to the increase in the size of an organ or tissue through the enlargement of its cells.
- **"Subcutaneous"**: "Sub-" means under or below, describing something situated or applied beneath the skin.
- **"Epigastric"**: "Epi-" indicates upon or above; refers to the abdominal region above the stomach.
- **"Antiseptic"**: "Anti-" denotes against; it refers to substances that prevent the growth of disease-causing microorganisms.
- **"Intramuscular"**: "Intra-" signifies within; referring to something occurring within or administered into a muscle.

- **"Interstitial"**: "Inter-" means between; it describes something occurring between the structures or spaces of the body, like interstitial fluid.
- **"Transfusion"**: "Trans-" indicates across; in medical terms, it refers to the transfer of blood or blood products from one person to another.
- **"Suprarenal"**: "Supra-" means above or over; referring to the adrenal glands located on top of the kidneys.
- **"Polyuria"**: "Poly-" signifies many or excessive; it refers to the production of abnormally large volumes of dilute urine.
- **"Neoplasm"**: "Neo-" indicates new; a neoplasm is a new growth of tissue serving no physiological function, commonly referred to as a tumor.
- **"Macrocyclic"**: "Macro-" denotes large; refers to large ring-like structures in chemistry, often used in describing certain types of antibiotics or other cyclic compounds.
- **"Microorganism"**: "Micro-" means small; referring to microscopic organisms such as bacteria, viruses, and fungi.
- **"Exocrine"**: "Exo-" indicates outside or outward; referring to glands that secrete their products externally to some surface, whether directly or through a duct.
- **"Retrograde"**: "Retro-" means backward; in medical terms, it can describe a movement in the direction opposite to normal, such as retrograde amnesia where the ability to recall past memories is lost.

These terms illustrate the diversity and specificity of medical language, highlighting how prefixes help convey detailed information about medical conditions and treatments in a concise manner.

Examples and Explanation

To deepen understanding, here are detailed explanations of several common medical prefixes:

- **"Sub-"**: This prefix means under or below, as seen in "subcutaneous," which refers to something located or applied under the skin.
- **"Hyper-"**: Denotes excess or more than normal, used in terms such as "hypertension," which means high blood pressure, indicating pressure that is above the normal range.
- **"Brady-"**: Means slow, used in "bradycardia," which refers to a slower than usual heart rate.
- **Super-"**: Indicates above, over, or excessive, as in "supernumerary," which refers to something that exceeds the usual number, like an extra digit or tooth.
- **"Ecto-"**: Means outside or external, used in "ectopic pregnancy," which refers to a pregnancy occurring outside the uterus, typically in a fallopian tube.
- **"Endo-"**: Denotes within or inside, as seen in "endoscopy," a procedure that involves inserting a camera inside the body to observe internal organs.
- **"Tachy-"**: Means fast, used in "tachypnea," which refers to abnormally rapid breathing.
- **"Dys-"**: Indicates bad, difficult, or abnormal, as in "dysphagia," which refers to difficulty swallowing.
- **"Eu-"**: Means good, normal, as seen in "eupnea," which refers to normal, good, unlabored breathing.
- **"Hemi-"**: Indicates half, used in "hemiplegia," which refers to paralysis of one side of the body.
- **"Mega-" or "Megalo-"**: Means large or enlarged, as in "megacolon," which refers to an abnormally enlarged colon.
- **"Multi-"**: Indicates many or multiple, as in

"multigravida," which refers to a woman who has been pregnant more than once.

- **"Pan-":** Means all or every, used in "pancytopenia," which refers to the reduction of all types of blood cells.
- **"Primi-":** Indicates first, as in "primipara," which refers to a woman who is giving birth for the first time.
- **"Pseudo-":** Means false, used in "pseudocyesis," a condition where a woman believes she is pregnant, showing signs of pregnancy but without an actual pregnancy.
- **"Re-":** Indicates again or back, as in "recurrent," which refers to something occurring repeatedly.
- **"Semi-":** Means half or partial, used in "semiconscious," where the individual is only partially conscious.
- **"Ultra-":** Indicates beyond, excessive, or more than usual, as seen in "ultrasound," a technique that uses high-frequency sound waves beyond the range of human hearing to create images of internal body structures.

These terms with their prefixes provide essential clues about the nature of medical conditions or procedures, enhancing the precision and efficiency of medical communication.

Practical Implications

Understanding and using prefixes correctly is vital in medical settings as they can significantly alter the meaning of the terms they modify. Misinterpretation can lead to incorrect treatment plans and patient care strategies. Thus, learning these prefixes enhances a healthcare professional's ability to engage in accurate and effective communication.

- **"Dys-"**: Indicates abnormal, difficult, or painful, used in "dysfunction," which generally means an abnormality or disturbance in function.
- **"Tachy-"**: Means fast, seen in "tachycardia," which describes a rapid heart rate.
- **"A-"/"An-"**: Denotes absence or lack, used in "anemia," which refers to a lack of red blood cells or hemoglobin in the blood, leading to fatigue and other symptoms.
- **"Auto-"**: Means self or same, used in "autoimmune," where the body's immune system attacks its own tissues.
- **"De-"**: Indicates removal or reversal, as seen in "decompression," which refers to the process of relieving pressure.
- **"Hyper-"**: Indicates over or excessive, used in "hyperactive," which describes excessive or pathological activity.
- **"Hypo-"**: Means under or below normal, as in "hypothermia," which refers to dangerously low body temperature.
- **"Inter-"**: Denotes between or among, used in "intervertebral," which refers to the space located between the vertebrae of the spine.
- **"Intra-"**: Indicates within or inside, as in "intravenous," meaning administered directly into the veins.
- **"Macro-"**: Means large, used in "macrocephaly," which refers to an abnormally large head.
- **"Micro-"**: Indicates small, as seen in "microscopic," which refers to something so small that it can only be seen with a microscope.
- **"Neo-"**: Means new, used in "neonate," referring to a newborn child, especially one less than four weeks old.
- **"Peri-"**: Denotes surrounding or around, used in "pericardium," which is the membrane enclosing the heart.

- **"Poly-"**: Indicates many, as in "polydactyly," which refers to the condition of having more than the usual number of fingers or toes.
- **"Post-"**: Means after, as seen in "postpartum," referring to the period of time after childbirth.
- **"Pre-"**: Indicates before, used in "prenatal," which refers to the period before birth.
- **"Sub-"**: Means under or below, as in "sublingual," referring to medication administered under the tongue.

These prefixes provide valuable insights into the condition or action described, helping medical professionals communicate effectively and precisely about health issues and treatments.

Educational Focus in Medical Studies

For students of medicine and related fields, a thorough knowledge of prefixes is not just about vocabulary building. It's about developing a deep understanding of the language that forms the bedrock of their future profession. This understanding facilitates more effective learning and application of medical concepts, and better preparation for patient interactions where clear and precise communication is crucial.

In summary, prefixes in medical terminology are not merely prefixes; they are keys that unlock deeper meanings and enhance understanding in the practice of medicine. Mastery of these elements is essential for anyone entering the medical field, contributing significantly to the accuracy and clarity of medical communication.

Suffixes in Medical Terminology

Suffixes in medical terminology are essential components that are affixed to the end of word roots to elaborate on the condition, action, diagnosis, or procedure associated with the medical term. These suffixes transform basic word roots into fully developed terms that healthcare professionals use in daily medical practice.

Definition and Importance

A suffix can often completely change the meaning of the word root to which it is attached, specifying whether the term describes a disease, a diagnostic procedure, a treatment method, or a pathological condition. For example:

- **"-itis"**: This suffix denotes inflammation, turning a root like "gastr-" (stomach) into "gastritis," which means inflammation of the stomach.
- **"-ectomy"**: Indicates surgical removal, transforming "appendix" into "appendectomy," the surgical removal of the appendix.
- **"-osis"**: Typically implies an abnormal condition or disease, as seen in "fibrosis," which refers to the development of fibrous connective tissue as a reparative response to injury or damage.
- **"-otomy"**: Indicates a cutting or surgical incision. For example, "tracheotomy" refers to a surgical procedure that creates an opening in the trachea (windpipe) to facilitate breathing.
- **"-algia"**: Denotes pain. "Neuralgia" refers to sharp, shocking pain that follows the path of a nerve and is due to irritation or damage to the nerve.
- **"-cyte"**: Means cell. "Leukocyte" refers to a white blood cell, a type of immune cell involved in protecting the body against both infectious disease and foreign invaders.
- **"-emia"**: Pertains to a blood condition. "Anemia" refers to a condition in which you lack enough healthy red blood cells to carry adequate oxygen to your body's tissues.
- **"-gen"**: Indicates something that produces or causes.

"Pathogen" refers to any organism that can produce disease.

- **"-lysis"**: Refers to the breakdown or destruction. "Hemolysis" denotes the destruction of red blood cells which leads to the release of hemoglobin from within the red blood cells into the blood plasma.
- **"-megaly"**: Indicates enlargement. "Hepatomegaly" refers to an abnormal enlargement of the liver.
- **"-oma"**: Indicates a tumor or growth. "Melanoma" refers to a tumor of melanin-forming cells, typically a malignant tumor associated with skin cancer.
- **"-pathy"**: Refers to disease or a disorder. "Myopathy" pertains to a muscular disease in which the muscle fibers do not function, resulting in muscular weakness.
- **"-plasty"**: Means surgical repair or reconstruction. "Rhinoplasty" refers to a cosmetic surgical procedure in the nose to change its shape or improve its function.
- **"-rrhea"**: Indicates flow or discharge. "Diarrhea" refers to the condition of having at least three loose, liquid, or watery bowel movements each day.
- **"-scope"**: Indicates an instrument for visual examination. "Endoscope" is a tool used in the procedure of endoscopy, a nonsurgical procedure used to examine a person's digestive tract using a flexible tube with a light and camera attached to it.

These suffixes are vital in the field of medicine as they not only help in diagnosing and treating but also in communicating precise medical information efficiently and effectively.

Usage in Clinical Settings

Suffixes are particularly valuable in clinical settings for several reasons:

- **Precision in Communication**: They help provide precise and concise descriptions of complex medical conditions and procedures, which is crucial for effective communication among healthcare professionals.
- **Diagnostic Clarity**: Suffixes often indicate specific diagnostic or pathological states, aiding in the classification of diseases and the determination of appropriate treatment plans.
- **Treatment Specifications**: By identifying specific procedures through suffixes, such as "-otomy" (cutting into or incision) or "-plasty" (surgical repair or reconstruction), medical staff can quickly understand the type of surgical intervention discussed.
- **Standardization Across Languages:** Suffixes in medical terminology help standardize medical language across different languages and cultures, which is crucial for international collaboration and understanding in the global healthcare community. This standardization ensures that medical professionals worldwide can comprehend and apply medical knowledge uniformly.
- **Facilitation of Learning:** Learning medical terms can be daunting due to their complexity and length. Suffixes categorize terms into understandable parts, making it easier for students and new healthcare professionals to memorize and recall medical vocabulary. For example, knowing that "-itis" means inflammation allows learners to recognize this condition across different medical terms.
- **Enhancement of Patient Communication:** By using well-defined medical suffixes, healthcare providers can more clearly explain diagnoses, treatments, and procedures to patients. This clarity improves patient understanding and engagement in their own care process. For instance, explaining that "arthroscopy" involves

viewing the inside of a joint helps patients understand what to expect from the procedure.

- **Legal and Documentation Accuracy:** In medical documentation and legal contexts, the precise use of medical terminology, influenced significantly by suffixes, ensures that patient records are accurate and legally sound. For example, the suffix "-ectomy" in "mastectomy" accurately conveys that the procedure involves the removal of the breast, which is crucial information in surgical consents and medical records.

- **Research and Development:** Suffixes in medical terms are crucial for researchers who need to accurately describe experimental procedures, clinical trials, and study outcomes. The precise language facilitated by suffixes helps in the formulation of research papers, grants, and presentations that are comprehensible to a broad scientific audience. For instance, terms like "neuroplasty" (reconstructive surgery of a nerve) or "angiogenesis" (formation of new blood vessels) clearly describe the focus of research studies.

Detailed Examples of Common Medical Suffixes

- **"-itis"** (inflammation): Used in terms such as "arthritis" (inflammation of the joints), "bronchitis" (inflammation of the bronchial tubes).
- **"-ectomy"** (removal): Found in terms like "cholecystectomy" (removal of the gallbladder), "mastectomy" (removal of a breast).
- **"-osis"** (condition, usually abnormal): Appears in terms such as "necrosis" (death of body tissue), "psychosis" (a severe mental disorder).

- **"-graphy"** (process of recording): Used in "angiography," a procedure to view blood vessels.
- **"-logy"** (study of): As in "dermatology" (study of the skin), "neurology" (study of the nervous system).
- **"-megaly"** (enlargement): Included in terms such as "cardiomegaly" (enlargement of the heart), "hepatomegaly" (enlargement of the liver).
- **"-pathy"** (disease or suffering): Found in "neuropathy" (disease or dysfunction of one or more peripheral nerves), "cardiomyopathy" (disease of the heart muscle).
- **"-scopy"** (to look, to see): Used in "endoscopy" (looking inside the body using an instrument), "colonoscopy" (examination of the colon).
- **"-therapy"** (treatment): As in "chemotherapy" (treatment of disease by chemical substances), "radiotherapy" (treatment using radiation).
- **"-phobia"** (fear): Used in "claustrophobia," which refers to an irrational fear of confined spaces.
- **"-plasia"** (formation, growth): Found in terms like "hyperplasia," which refers to the increased growth of cells within a specific tissue, causing the tissue to increase in size.
- **"-cele"** (hernia, swelling): Appears in terms such as "cystocele," which is a condition where the bladder herniates into the vaginal wall.
- **"-penia"** (deficiency): Used in "leukopenia," which refers to a decrease in the number of white blood cells in the blood, often affecting immune response.
- **"-rrhage"** or **"-rrhagia"** (excessive flow or discharge): As seen in "hemorrhage," which refers to excessive bleeding.
- **"-plegia"** (paralysis): Included in terms such as "paraplegia," which refers to paralysis affecting the lower half of the body typically including both legs.

- **"-rrhea"** (flow, discharge): Found in "diarrhea," which refers to the condition of having loose or liquid bowel movements frequently.
- **"-stasis"** (stopping, controlling): Used in "hemostasis," which refers to the process of stopping bleeding or the flow of blood.
- **"-trophy"** (nutrition, growth): As in "atrophy," which refers to the partial or complete wasting away of a part of the body.
- **"-iasis"** (process, state): Appears in "psoriasis," a chronic skin disease characterized by red patches covered with white scales.

Each of these suffixes adds specific meaning to the root word it complements, helping medical professionals to describe and communicate complex medical concepts accurately.

Educational Implications

For students and professionals in healthcare, understanding and using suffixes correctly is not just a matter of linguistic proficiency but is essential for accurate diagnosis, treatment, and communication. Mastery of medical suffixes enhances the ability to quickly understand medical literature, communicate conditions and procedures accurately, and participate in clinical discussions with confidence.

Suffixes in medical terminology play a pivotal role in the precise and effective communication of medical information. They are fundamental in turning basic linguistic elements into comprehensive terms that describe medical phenomena in detail, making them indispensable tools in the medical community.

Combining Forms

Combining forms play a crucial role in medical terminology, acting as a bridge that connects word roots, prefixes, and suffixes to form coherent and pronounceable medical terms. They are instrumental in ensuring that medical language remains precise yet fluid, allowing healthcare professionals to communicate with clarity and accuracy.

Function and Utility of Combining Forms in Medical Terminology

Combining forms in medical terminology serve a critical function by ensuring the phonetic coherence and ease of pronunciation of complex medical terms. This linguistic strategy involves appending a vowel, typically "o," but sometimes "i" or "a," to a word root. This additional vowel acts as a phonetic bridge, facilitating smoother transitions between sounds that might otherwise clash or be difficult to articulate. This adjustment is particularly vital in the field of medicine, where the precision of communication can directly impact patient care and medical outcomes.

How Combining Forms Work

The vowel added through combining forms primarily functions as a buffer. It alleviates the awkwardness that might arise from the juxtaposition of consonants when different roots, prefixes, or suffixes are merged to form a single term. For example, without the combining vowel, a term like 'gastroenterology' would be clunkier and more challenging to pronounce ('gastrenterology'). The insertion of the "o" after "gastr-" and before "enter-" smooths the transition and maintains the flow of speech, making the term easier to pronounce and remember.

Importance in Medical Communication

In medical contexts, where terms can be exceptionally long and complex due to the need to incorporate multiple descriptive elements, these combining forms prevent miscommunication. They also standardize terms across different languages, as many are derived from Greek and Latin. This universality is crucial because it allows medical professionals worldwide to understand and use these terms consistently, regardless of their native language or where they were trained.

Linguistic Flexibility and Learning

Combining forms not only facilitate easier communication and comprehension but also enhance learning and recall. By breaking down complex medical terms into simpler, more digestible parts, medical students and professionals can more easily master the vast vocabulary required in their field. The consistent use of a vowel like "o" provides a predictable pattern that aids in the mental organization of medical information, thereby supporting more effective education and faster assimilation of knowledge.

Broader Implications for Medical Practice

The utility of combining forms extends beyond just easing pronunciation—they ensure that the terminology used in diagnostics, treatment plans, and scientific research is accurately understood and applied. This precision is crucial for documenting medical records, writing prescription orders, and communicating diagnoses and treatment plans among interdisciplinary teams. Without such clarity provided by combining forms, the risk of errors could increase, potentially impacting patient safety and the effectiveness of medical interventions.

Usage in Medical Communication

Combining forms are not merely linguistic conveniences; they enhance the functionality of medical communication by enabling the construction of words that are not only precise but also easier to understand and articulate.

- **Medical Documentation**: In written medical communication, combining forms prevent misinterpretation of terms and ensure that the documentation is clear and standardized, which is crucial for maintaining patient records and communicating among specialists.

- **Educational Purposes**: For students of medicine, learning combining forms is foundational because it helps in understanding and remembering medical terminology by breaking down complex terms into digestible parts.
- **Clinical Discussions:** Combining forms facilitate clear and concise verbal exchanges between healthcare providers during clinical consultations and discussions, ensuring that complex information is conveyed accurately and quickly.
- **Interdisciplinary Communication:** In environments where multiple specialties interact, such as hospitals, combining forms help standardize terminology so that specialists from different fields can understand each other more effectively.
- **Pharmaceutical Uses:** In pharmacology, combining forms are used to denote drugs and their actions, which helps in the precise description of pharmacodynamics and pharmacokinetics in medication management.
- **Medical Coding:** For medical billing and coding, combining forms are essential for creating the specific codes used in healthcare documentation, which are crucial for insurance claims and administrative tasks.
- **Patient Education:** Healthcare providers use combining forms to break down intimidating medical jargon when explaining diagnoses and treatments to patients, thereby enhancing patient understanding and engagement in their care.
- **Telemedicine:** As telehealth platforms become more prevalent, combining forms ensure that verbal and written communications are clear and concise, which is vital for delivering remote care effectively.

- **Research and Publications:** Medical researchers use combining forms to write precise and comprehensible research papers, abstracts, and presentations, facilitating knowledge dissemination within the scientific community.
- **Multilingual Translation:** Combining forms aid in the translation of medical texts between languages, maintaining the accuracy of technical terms and ensuring that translations adhere to international medical standards.
- **Legal Documentation:** In legal contexts, precise medical terminology underpinned by combining forms is crucial for the documentation of medical malpractice, consent forms, and other legal documents in healthcare.
- **Health Informatics:** In the field of health informatics, combining forms help in the development and maintenance of medical databases and software that rely on standardized medical terminology to process and store information efficiently.

Examples and Applications

Here are detailed explanations of some common combining forms used in medical terminology:

- **"Osteo-arthritis"**: In this term, "osteo-" refers to bone, and "-arthritis" indicates inflammation of the joint. The combining form "osteo-" connects smoothly with "-arthritis," facilitating a clear and pronounceable term that indicates inflammation involving bone structures of the joint.
- **"Gastroenterology"**: This term is a combination of three elements: "gastro-" (stomach), "entero-" (intestine), and

"-logy" (study of). The combining forms "gastro-" and "entero-" are linked through their vowels, making the complex field of study dealing with the stomach and intestines not only more pronounceable but also logically segmented.

- **"Electroencephalogram"**: Here, "electro-" (electricity), "encephalo-" (brain), and "-gram" (record) are joined using the combining form "encephalo-". This term describes the recording of electrical activity in the brain, illustrating how combining forms help describe detailed medical diagnostics.

- **"Hemato-oncology"**: Combining "hemato-" (blood) and "oncology" (study of tumors) exemplifies how combining forms link areas of medical specialization, in this case, the study of blood-related cancers.

- **"Cardiomyopathy"**: In this example, "cardio-" (heart) and "-myopathy" (muscle disease) merge to describe diseases of the heart muscle, highlighting the condition's specific location and nature in one coherent term.

- **"Dermatopathology"**: This term combines "dermato-" (skin) and "pathology" (study of disease) to refer to the study of skin diseases at a microscopic level, highlighting specific skin conditions and their pathological aspects.

- **"Neuroophthalmology"**: Combining "neuro-" (nerve) and "ophthalmology" (study of eyes) to describe a specialized field focused on diseases that affect the optic nerve and the visual pathways of the brain.

- **"Gastroenterology"**: Utilizes "gastro-" (stomach), "entero-" (intestines), and "-logy" (study of) to describe the branch of medicine focusing on the digestive system and its disorders.

- **"Rhinoplasty"**: Combines "rhino-" (nose) and "-plasty" (surgical repair or reconstruction) to describe a type of surgery performed to change the shape of the nose for cosmetic or medical reasons.

- **"Angioplasty"**: Uses "angio-" (vessel) and "-plasty" (surgical repair) to describe a procedure that mechanically widens narrowed or obstructed blood vessels, typically to treat arterial atherosclerosis.
- **"Hepatology"**: Combines "hepato-" (liver) and "-logy" (study of) to denote the branch of medicine concerned with the study, diagnosis, treatment, and prevention of diseases affecting the liver.
- **"Arthroscopy"**: Utilizes "arthro-" (joint) and "-scopy" (to look) to describe a surgical procedure for diagnosing and treating joint problems by visualizing the joint area with a camera.
- **"Psychoneuroendocrinology"**: Combines "psycho-" (mind), "neuro-" (nerve), "endo-" (within), and "crinology" (study of hormones) to describe the study of how the mind's psychological processes affect the nervous and endocrine system functions.
- **"Otorhinolaryngology"**: Links "oto-" (ear), "rhino-" (nose), and "laryngo-" (throat) with "-logy" (study of), describing a medical specialty focused on the ears, nose, and throat.
- **"Phlebotomy"**: Combines "phlebo-" (vein) and "-tomy" (cutting), referring to the act or practice of opening a vein by incision or puncture to draw blood as part of a medical testing process.
- **"Cytotechnology"**: Uses "cyto-" (cell) and "technology" to describe a laboratory field that studies cells and cellular anomalies, mainly to diagnose cancers and other diseases.
- **"Laparoscopy"**: This term brings together "laparo-" (abdomen) and "-scopy" (to look) to describe a minimally

invasive surgical diagnostic procedure used to examine organs inside the abdomen.

Combining forms are integral to medical terminology, ensuring that terms are not only technically accurate but also practically useful. They facilitate seamless and clear communication within the medical community, aid in the education of medical professionals, and ensure that patient care documentation is unambiguous. Mastery of combining forms is essential for anyone involved in healthcare, as it underpins effective communication and enhances the understanding of complex medical concepts.

As we conclude Chapter 1, it's evident that a solid grasp of medical terminology's foundational elements is crucial for anyone pursuing a career in healthcare. Word roots, prefixes, suffixes, and combining forms not only provide the building blocks of the complex language used in medicine but also enhance communication, learning, and operational efficiency within the medical community. These elements are integral to creating terms that accurately describe various medical conditions, diagnostics, and treatments, thus bridging the gap between different languages and disciplines within the field.

The function of word roots as the core elements of medical words, prefixes that modify these roots, suffixes that indicate procedures or conditions, and combining forms that ensure phonetic harmony, have all been explored in detail. Mastery of these components allows healthcare professionals to communicate with precision and clarity, reducing the likelihood of errors in patient care and increasing the efficacy of medical services. For students, these fundamentals serve as a gateway to deeper understanding and application of medical knowledge, supporting their educational journey and future professional practice.

Through examples like "osteoporosis," "electroencephalogram," and "gastroenterology," we see how each component plays a role in elucidating the function and purpose of medical terms. These examples not only illustrate the practical application of combining forms but also highlight the necessity of understanding the nuances that each segment—prefix, root, and suffix—brings to the term's overall meaning.

Moreover, the systematic study of these elements empowers medical practitioners to keep pace with evolving medical language and the continuous introduction of new terms resulting from advances in medical science. It is this dynamic nature of medical terminology that makes its study both challenging and essential.

As we transition from the basics of medical language to Chapter 2, we will dive into the Body Systems, where the foundational knowledge from Chapter 1 will be applied to specific anatomical and physiological contexts. This next chapter will explore how medical terminology is used to describe the intricate and interrelated systems of the human body, from the skeletal system to the nervous system and beyond.

Each section of Chapter 2 will focus on a different body system, examining the common medical terms associated with that system's anatomy and pathophysiology. Diagrams and detailed descriptions will aid in visualizing and understanding the complex interactions within and between these systems. This approach not only enriches the learner's vocabulary but also enhances their ability to apply this knowledge in real-world medical settings.

Chapter 2 will build on the linguistic foundations established in the first chapter, extending the discussion to the practical and detailed examination of body systems. It promises to be an essential continuation for anyone committed to mastering medical terminology in the context of comprehensive human health and disease.

Chapter 2
Body Systems
Introduction

In Chapter 2, we delve into the intricate network of body systems that underpin human physiology. Each system plays a unique role, contributing to the overall health and functionality of the body. This comprehensive exploration will cover each system in detail, discussing its structure, function, and the medical terminology associated with it. Through a systematic approach, this chapter aims to provide students and healthcare professionals with the foundational knowledge necessary to understand and discuss human anatomy and common medical conditions effectively.

Skeletal System

The skeletal system provides the structural framework for the human body, protects vital organs, and facilitates movement in conjunction with the muscular system. It consists of bones, joints, cartilage, and ligaments. Medical terminology related to the skeletal system includes terms for various bone types, joint mechanics, and common conditions such as fractures, osteoporosis, and arthritis. Understanding these terms helps in diagnosing bone injuries and diseases, discussing treatments, and appreciating the biomechanics of movement.

Muscular System

The muscular system is responsible for body movements, posture, and heat production through muscle contractions. It comprises three types of muscle tissue: skeletal, cardiac, and smooth. This section will explore the terminology related to muscle anatomy, the function of different muscle types, and disorders like muscular dystrophy and strains. Mastery of this terminology is essential for discussing procedures that involve muscle manipulation and understanding muscular pathologies.

Cardiovascular System

The cardiovascular system circulates blood throughout the body, delivering oxygen and nutrients to tissues and removing waste products. This section covers the anatomy of the heart and blood vessels, along with terms related to blood circulation and common cardiovascular diseases such as hypertension and coronary artery disease. Familiarity with these terms is crucial for any medical professional involved in cardiac care or any health specialties that require understanding of vascular health.

Respiratory System

The respiratory system manages the exchange of gases between the body and the environment, making it crucial for cellular respiration. In this section, we will discuss the terminology related to lung anatomy, the mechanics of breathing, and common respiratory conditions like asthma, COPD, and pneumonia. Understanding these terms enables healthcare providers to communicate effectively about respiratory assessments and treatments.

Nervous System

The nervous system regulates body functions and processes information from both internal and external environments. This section introduces terms related to the central and peripheral nervous systems, brain structures, neural pathways, and neurological disorders such as epilepsy and multiple sclerosis. This knowledge is vital for professionals dealing with neurological evaluations and treatments.

Digestive System

The digestive system breaks down food, absorbs nutrients, and eliminates waste. This section will explain terminology associated with the gastrointestinal tract, including the stomach, intestines, and accessory organs like the liver and pancreas. It also covers digestive disorders, such as GERD and Crohn's disease. Proficiency in this area is necessary for professionals focusing on nutrition, gastroenterology, and general health care.

Endocrine System

The endocrine system consists of glands that produce and secrete hormones. It regulates various bodily functions, including metabolism, growth, and mood. The terminology covered includes hormone names, glandular functions, and endocrine disorders like diabetes and thyroid imbalances. Understanding this system is crucial for endocrinologists and all health professionals who manage hormonal therapies.

Urinary System

The urinary system removes waste from the body and maintains blood's chemical balance. Key terms in this section involve the kidneys, bladder, and the process of urination, along with conditions like urinary tract infections and kidney stones. Knowledge of this system is essential for urologists and healthcare workers in nephrology and general medicine.

Reproductive Systems

The reproductive systems include male and female anatomical structures and processes involved in reproduction. This section covers terms related to the anatomy of both systems, reproductive health, and common conditions like infertility and prostate enlargement. Understanding these terms is vital for professionals in gynecology, obstetrics, and urology.

Integumentary System

The integumentary system includes the skin, hair, nails, and glands. It protects against environmental hazards, regulates temperature, and provides sensory information. This section will discuss terminology related to skin anatomy, functions, and disorders like eczema and skin cancer. Dermatologists and all health professionals require a thorough understanding of this system.

Lymphatic and Immune Systems

The lymphatic and immune systems defend against infectious disease and maintain bodily fluids' balance. Terms related to lymphatic vessels, lymph nodes, and immune responses, along with conditions like lymphedema and autoimmune diseases, will be discussed. Knowledge of these systems is crucial for professionals in immunology, infectious diseases, and general healthcare.

Each of these systems is complex and vital to the body's health and functionality. By understanding the specific terminology associated with each system, healthcare professionals can enhance their diagnostic and treatment capabilities, providing better patient care and engaging in more meaningful scientific discussions.

Comprehensive Exploration of the Skeletal System

Introduction to the Skeletal System

The skeletal system is an integral component of the human body, serving several vital functions that go beyond mere structural support. Comprising approximately 206 bones in the adult human body, along with joints, cartilage, and ligaments, the skeletal system provides the framework that supports and shapes the body, protects internal organs, stores essential minerals like calcium and phosphorus, and facilitates movement by working in concert with the muscular system. Understanding the terminology and functionality of the skeletal system is crucial for professionals in medicine, orthopedics, and related fields.

Structure of the Skeletal System

The skeletal system can be broadly classified into two main parts: the axial skeleton and the appendicular skeleton. The **axial skeleton** consists of the skull, vertebral column, and rib cage, which primarily support the central axis of the body and protect the brain, spinal cord, and vital organs within the thorax. The **appendicular skeleton** includes the bones of the upper and lower limbs, shoulders, and pelvis, facilitating movement and interaction with the environment.

- **Bones**: Each bone in the skeletal system can be categorized as a long, short, flat, or irregular bone, depending on its shape and the specific function it serves. For example, long bones like the femur and humerus are crucial for creating movement, while flat bones like those of the skull provide protection for vital organs.
- **Joints**: Joints are the functional units of mobility in the skeletal system where two or more bones meet. Joints are classified based on their structure and the movement they allow, including synovial (freely movable), fibrous (little to no movement), and cartilaginous (limited movement) joints.
- **Cartilage and Ligaments**: Cartilage provides a cushion between bones and reduces friction in joints, aiding in smooth movement. Ligaments are tough, elastic bands of connective tissue that stabilize joints by connecting bones to each other.

Function of the Skeletal System

The primary functions of the skeletal system include:

- **Support**: Bones provide a rigid framework that supports the body's shape and form.
- **Protection**: Bony structures like the skull and rib cage protect vital organs from external impacts.
- **Movement**: Bones act as levers and fulcrums, upon which muscles act to produce movement.
- **Mineral Storage**: Bones store minerals, primarily

calcium and phosphorus, which can be released into the bloodstream as needed.

- **Blood Cell Production**: The bone marrow, found within the hollow centers of many bones, is the site of red blood cell production.

Medical Terminology in the Skeletal System

To effectively communicate about the skeletal system, several key terms need to be understood:

- **Osteo-**: A prefix relating to the bones, used in terms like osteoporosis (a condition characterized by porous and weakened bones) and osteoarthritis (inflammation and degeneration of joint cartilage and the underlying bone).
- **Fracture**: A break in the continuity of a bone. Fractures can be classified into several types, such as transverse, spiral, and comminuted, depending on the nature of the break.
- **Arthritis**: A term used to describe over 100 types of joint diseases that cause symptoms such as inflammation, pain, and stiffness.
- **Kyphosis**, **Lordosis**, **Scoliosis**: Terms used to describe types of spinal curvatures that can impact posture and movement.

Common Conditions Affecting the Skeletal System

Several disorders can affect the skeletal system, impacting its ability to perform its functions effectively:

- **Fractures**: Often caused by high force impact or stress, or due to bone weakness from conditions like osteoporosis.
- **Arthritis**: Including osteoarthritis and rheumatoid

arthritis, involving inflammation of the joints, leading to pain and functional impairments.
- **Osteoporosis**: A disease where decreased bone strength increases the risk of a broken bone.

Understanding the skeletal system's complex structure and functions is fundamental for diagnosing and treating disorders effectively. The terminology associated with this system provides the tools needed by healthcare professionals to describe conditions accurately, communicate diagnoses, and implement effective treatments. Through systematic study and practical application, students and professionals can appreciate the biomechanics of movement and the intricacies of human anatomy linked to the skeletal system. This foundational knowledge is crucial for those aiming to specialize in fields such as orthopedics, physical therapy, and sports medicine.

Comprehensive Exploration of the Muscular System
Introduction to the Muscular System

The muscular system is a complex network of tissues that plays a crucial role in the overall functioning of the human body. Comprising more than 600 muscles, the system is responsible for movements ranging from voluntary motions like walking and running to involuntary actions such as heartbeats and digestive processes. This chapter will delve into the types of muscle tissues, their functions, and the essential terminology needed to understand and discuss the anatomy and pathologies of the muscular system effectively.

Types of Muscle Tissue

The muscular system includes three distinct types of muscle tissue, each with specialized functions:

- **Skeletal Muscle**: These muscles are attached to bones and are responsible for voluntary movements. They are striated, meaning they have a banded appearance, and are controlled consciously by the nervous system.
- **Cardiac Muscle**: Found exclusively in the walls of the heart, this type of muscle contracts involuntarily to pump blood throughout the body. Like skeletal muscle, it is striated, but it operates autonomously with regulation from the nervous and endocrine systems.
- **Smooth Muscle**: This type is found in the walls of hollow organs (like intestines and blood vessels) and is non-striated. Smooth muscle contractions are involuntary and help to regulate functions such as blood flow and digestion.

Function of the Muscular System

The primary functions of the muscular system include:

- **Movement**: Muscles work in response to stimulation from the nervous system, contracting to cause movement.
- **Posture and Stability**: Muscles contract slightly even at rest, which helps maintain posture and balance.
- **Heat Production**: Muscle contractions produce heat as a by-product, helping to maintain body temperature.

Medical Terminology in the Muscular System

Understanding the terminology associated with the muscular system is vital for medical professionals, particularly when diagnosing conditions or planning treatments involving muscle manipulation. Key terms include:

- **Myopathy**: Refers to any disease of the muscle that can disrupt its function.

- **Myalgia**: Means muscle pain and is a common symptom in many muscular disorders.
- **Myositis**: Indicates inflammation of the muscle tissue.
- **Atrophy**: Refers to the wasting away or reduction in muscle size, which can occur from disuse or underlying medical conditions.
- **Hypertrophy**: Describes an increase in muscle size, typically as a result of physical training.

Common Disorders of the Muscular System

Muscular disorders can significantly impact quality of life by limiting movement and causing pain. Some common muscular disorders include:

- **Muscular Dystrophy**: A group of inherited diseases that cause progressive weakness and loss of muscle mass.
- **Strains**: Often called pulled muscles, these are injuries to the muscle or the tendons that attach muscles to bones, typically caused by overuse or acute injury.
- **Tetanus**: A serious bacterial disease that affects the body's muscles and nerves, leading to severe muscle spasms.

The muscular system is fundamental to nearly all bodily functions, from locomotion and posture maintenance to vital involuntary activities like pumping blood. A thorough understanding of the muscle tissues, their functions, and related medical terminology is indispensable for healthcare professionals engaged in treating muscular diseases and injuries. Mastery of this system's intricacies not only aids in effective treatment planning but also enhances the ability to educate patients about their conditions and the care needed to manage or resolve muscular issues. As we continue to explore the body systems in subsequent chapters, the interconnectivity between the muscular system and other systems will become increasingly evident, highlighting the integrated nature of human physiology.

Comprehensive Exploration of the Cardiovascular System

Introduction to the Cardiovascular System

The cardiovascular system, also known as the circulatory system, is pivotal in maintaining the life-sustaining process of blood circulation throughout the body. It consists of the heart, blood vessels, and blood itself. This system's primary function is to deliver oxygen and nutrients to every cell, remove waste products, and aid in various body processes, such as temperature regulation and disease protection. This chapter will delve into the detailed anatomy of the cardiovascular components, the mechanics of blood circulation, and the crucial medical terminology necessary to understand and discuss cardiovascular health and diseases.

Anatomy of the Cardiovascular System

The heart, the central organ of the cardiovascular system, functions as a pump to circulate blood through two primary circuits: the pulmonary circuit and the systemic circuit. The heart is divided into four chambers: two upper atria and two lower ventricles. Key structures include:

- **Arteries**: Vessels that carry oxygen-rich blood away from the heart to the tissues.
- **Veins**: Vessels that return oxygen-depleted blood back to the heart.
- **Capillaries**: Tiny vessels where the exchange of water, oxygen, carbon dioxide, and many other nutrients and waste substances occurs between blood and tissues.

Function of the Cardiovascular System

The essential functions of this system encompass:

- **Circulation of Blood**: Ensuring continuous movement of blood throughout the body, delivering essential substances to cells and removing waste products.
- **Regulation of Blood Supply**: Adjusting the blood flow based on the body's needs, ensuring optimal performance during various activities and maintaining homeostasis.
- **Protection**: The circulatory system plays a critical role in the body's immune response and in clotting, which prevents excessive bleeding.

Medical Terminology in the Cardiovascular System

Mastery of specific cardiovascular terminology is essential for professionals involved in diagnosing and treating heart and vascular diseases. Important terms include:

- **Cardiomyopathy**: A term describing diseases of the heart muscle that affect cardiac function.
- **Atherosclerosis**: The buildup of fats, cholesterol, and other substances in and on the artery walls, which can restrict blood flow.
- **Arrhythmia**: An irregular heartbeat—either too fast, too slow, or erratic.
- **Ischemia**: A condition where blood flow (and thus oxygen) is restricted or reduced in a part of the body.
- **Hypertension**: High blood pressure, a condition in which the force of the blood against the artery walls is too high.

Common Cardiovascular Diseases

Cardiovascular diseases are among the leading causes of death globally. Understanding these conditions is vital for effective prevention, diagnosis, and management:

- **Coronary Artery Disease (CAD)**: Characterized by damaged or diseased coronary arteries, mainly due to plaque accumulation that narrows the arteries, reducing blood flow to the heart.
- **Myocardial Infarction (Heart Attack)**: Occurs when blood flow to a part of the heart is blocked for a long enough time that part of the heart muscle is damaged or dies.
- **Stroke**: A condition where the blood supply to part of the brain is interrupted or reduced, preventing brain tissue from getting oxygen and nutrients.

The cardiovascular system is complex yet integral to every function of the body. Comprehensive knowledge of this system's anatomy, function, and related medical terminology is crucial for any healthcare provider, especially those specializing in cardiac care. Understanding the terms and mechanisms discussed will enable medical professionals to better communicate about cardiovascular conditions, enhance patient care, and contribute effectively to the broader medical community's efforts to manage and mitigate heart-related illnesses. As we proceed to explore other body systems, the interaction of the cardiovascular system with these systems will further illustrate the interconnected nature of human physiology.

Comprehensive Exploration of the Respiratory System
Introduction to the Respiratory System

The respiratory system is fundamental to life, enabling the vital exchange of gases—oxygen and carbon dioxide—between the body and the environment. This system not only supports cellular respiration, which is crucial for energy production but also plays significant roles in maintaining the body's pH balance and in vocalization. This chapter will explore the anatomy of the respiratory system, delve into the mechanics of breathing, and discuss the medical terminology essential for understanding and treating respiratory conditions.

Anatomy of the Respiratory System

The respiratory system is primarily composed of the airways, the lungs, and the respiratory muscles. The airways include the nose, pharynx, larynx, trachea, bronchi, and bronchioles, which guide air to and from the lungs. The lungs are the central organs where gas exchange occurs, housed within the rib cage and protected by the rib bones. The diaphragm and intercostal muscles play critical roles in the mechanics of breathing by creating changes in pressure that allow air to flow in and out of the lungs.

- **Lungs**: The main organs where oxygen is absorbed into the bloodstream, and carbon dioxide is released from the bloodstream into the environment.
- **Bronchi and Bronchioles**: These airways branch from the trachea into progressively smaller tubes, directing air into the lungs.
- **Alveoli**: Tiny sacs within the lungs where gas exchange occurs through their thin walls adjacent to capillaries.

Function of the Respiratory System

The primary function of the respiratory system includes:

- **Gas Exchange**: This is the core function, where oxygen is inhaled into the lungs and carbon dioxide is expelled, supporting cellular metabolism throughout the body.
- **Regulation of Blood pH**: By adjusting the rate of CO_2 removal, the respiratory system helps maintain

acidic-basic balance in the body, which is vital for normal bodily functions.

- **Protection**: The respiratory system protects against pathogens and particulates through various mechanisms like the nasal hairs, mucus production, and cough reflex.

Medical Terminology in the Respiratory System

Understanding the specific terminology associated with respiratory anatomy and pathology is crucial for effective clinical communication. Some key terms include:

- **Apnea**: The absence of breathing.
- **Dyspnea**: Difficult or labored breathing, often experienced as shortness of breath.
- **Tachypnea**: Abnormally rapid breathing.
- **Bronchitis**: Inflammation of the bronchial tubes.
- **Emphysema**: A condition where the alveoli are damaged, affecting the lungs' ability to expel air.

Common Respiratory Conditions

Respiratory diseases can significantly impact health and quality of life. This section addresses common conditions such as:

- **Asthma**: A chronic disease characterized by recurrent attacks of breathlessness and wheezing, which vary in severity and frequency from person to person.
- **Chronic Obstructive Pulmonary Disease (COPD)**: A group of lung conditions that block airflow and make breathing difficult.
- **Pneumonia**: An infection that inflames the air sacs in one or both lungs, which may fill with fluid or pus.

The respiratory system's complexity and its critical role in human physiology necessitate a thorough understanding of its structure, function, and the diseases that can affect it. For healthcare providers, mastery of the relevant medical terminology and an understanding of respiratory mechanics are essential to diagnose, discuss, and treat respiratory conditions effectively. This knowledge is also crucial for advising on preventive measures and lifestyle choices that can impact respiratory health. As we progress further into the study of body systems, the interdependence between the respiratory system and other systems, such as the cardiovascular system, will further illustrate the holistic nature of human biology.

Comprehensive Exploration of the Nervous System
Introduction to the Nervous System

The nervous system is an extensive, intricate network that orchestrates the body's activities by processing sensory information, regulating bodily functions, and facilitating cognition and communication. It is divided into the central nervous system (CNS), comprising the brain and spinal cord, and the peripheral nervous system (PNS), which includes all other neural elements. This chapter delves into the anatomy and function of these components, the neural pathways that connect them, and the common neurological disorders that can impact these systems.

Anatomy of the Nervous System

The **central nervous system (CNS)** acts as the control center for the body, interpreting sensory information and issuing instructions based on past experiences and current conditions. The **peripheral nervous system (PNS)** extends beyond the CNS to the limbs and organs, essentially serving as a communication relay back and forth between the brain and the extremities. It is further divided into the somatic nervous system, which controls voluntary movements, and the autonomic nervous system, which controls involuntary responses.

- **Brain**: The brain is the command center, located in the skull and functioning as the locus of thought, emotion, and executive control.
- **Spinal Cord**: Acts as a conduit for signals between the brain and the rest of the body, also hosting reflex actions independently of the brain.
- **Nerves**: Composed of neurons, nerves carry signals to and from the CNS to the rest of the body, facilitating quick and coordinated responses.

Function of the Nervous System

The nervous system has several critical functions:

- **Information Processing**: It processes vast amounts of information every second from sensory organs and internal systems.
- **Coordination and Control**: It coordinates voluntary and involuntary actions, such as movement, digestion, and heart rate.
- **Cognitive Functions**: It is central to cognitive functions like thinking, learning, memory, and decision-making.

Medical Terminology in the Nervous System

An understanding of specific medical terminology is crucial for professionals engaged in neurology and psychiatry. Essential terms include:

- **Neuroplasticity**: The ability of the nervous system to adapt and change as a result of experience or injury.
- **Neuropathy**: Any disease or dysfunction of peripheral nerves causing numbness or weakness.
- **Neurotransmitters**: Chemicals that transmit signals across a synapse from one neuron to another.

- **Synapse**: A junction between two nerve cells, where impulses pass by diffusion of neurotransmitters.

Common Neurological Disorders

Various disorders can affect the nervous system, each with potential impacts on health and quality of life:

- **Epilepsy**: A disorder in which nerve cell activity in the brain is disturbed, causing seizures.
- **Multiple Sclerosis (MS)**: A disease in which the immune system eats away at the protective covering of nerves, disrupting communication between the brain and the body.
- **Parkinson's Disease**: A progressive nervous system disorder that affects movement, causing tremors, stiffness, and slowing of movement.

The nervous system is fundamental to all functions of the human body, from regulating heartbeat and breathing to enabling the complex behaviors seen in human beings, such as cognition, emotion, and consciousness. Mastery of the nervous system's structures, functions, and related medical terminology is essential for any healthcare provider involved in neurological or psychiatric care. Understanding these aspects allows medical professionals to better diagnose, treat, and manage neurological disorders, contributing to improved patient outcomes and advancing our understanding of human biology. As we proceed through other body systems in subsequent chapters, the critical interactions between the nervous system and these systems will underscore the interconnectedness of all bodily functions.

Comprehensive Exploration of the Digestive System

Introduction to the Digestive System

The digestive system is a complex network of organs and glands that processes food, extracts and absorbs nutrients, and eliminates waste. It involves a coordinated series of mechanical and chemical actions that break down food into components that can be used by the body. Understanding the anatomy of the digestive system, the functions of its various parts, and the medical terminology associated with it is crucial for healthcare professionals involved in gastroenterology, nutrition, and general healthcare.

Anatomy of the Digestive System

The digestive tract, also known as the gastrointestinal (GI) tract, begins at the mouth and extends through the esophagus, stomach, small intestine, and large intestine, concluding at the rectum and anus. Each component plays a specific role in digestion:

- **Mouth**: Digestion begins here as food is chewed and mixed with saliva, which contains enzymes that start breaking down carbohydrates.
- **Esophagus**: Acts as a conduit for moving swallowed food and liquids from the throat to the stomach.
- **Stomach**: Secretes acid and enzymes that continue the process of breaking down food into a more digestible form.
- **Small Intestine**: The primary site for nutrient absorption. Enzymes from the pancreas and bile from the liver aid in digesting fats, proteins, and carbohydrates.
- **Large Intestine**: Absorbs water and salts from the material that has not been digested as food, and is thus transformed into solid waste for elimination.
- **Accessory Organs**: Include the liver, pancreas, and gallbladder, which produce enzymes and bile that aid in digestion but are not part of the GI tract itself.

Function of the Digestive System

The digestive system's primary functions include:

- **Digestion**: Mechanical and chemical processes break down food into molecules small enough to be absorbed.
- **Absorption**: Nutrients from digested food are absorbed in the intestines and transported to other parts of the body to be used for energy, growth, and cell repair.
- **Elimination**: Removal of indigestible substances and waste products from the body in the form of feces.

Medical Terminology in the Digestive System

Proficiency in digestive system terminology is essential for diagnosing and treating gastrointestinal disorders effectively. Key terms include:

- **Gastroesophageal Reflux Disease (GERD)**: A digestive disorder that affects the lower esophageal sphincter, leading to acid reflux and heartburn.
- **Crohn's Disease**: A type of inflammatory bowel disease (IBD) that may affect any part of the gastrointestinal tract from mouth to anus.
- **Peptic Ulcer**: Sores that develop on the inner lining of the stomach and upper portion of the small intestine.
- **Hepatitis**: Inflammation of the liver, often caused by viral infections, that affects its ability to function.

Common Digestive Disorders

Various disorders can affect the digestive system, impacting digestion and overall health:

- **Irritable Bowel Syndrome (IBS)**: A common disorder that affects the large intestine, causing cramping, abdominal pain, bloating, gas, diarrhea, and constipation.

- **Pancreatitis**: Inflammation of the pancreas that occurs when digestive enzymes start digesting the pancreas itself.
- **Gallstones**: Hard deposits formed in the gallbladder that can block the flow of bile, causing pain, nausea, and potential complications.

The digestive system is essential for maintaining overall health by ensuring the body receives the necessary nutrients while eliminating waste. An in-depth understanding of this system's structure, function, and associated medical conditions is critical for healthcare providers. This knowledge not only aids in diagnosing and treating gastrointestinal diseases but also enhances the ability to advise patients on nutrition and preventive care measures. As we progress in studying the body systems, the relationship between the digestive system and other bodily functions, such as the endocrine and immune systems, will be highlighted, demonstrating the integrated nature of human physiology.

Comprehensive Exploration of the Endocrine System
Introduction to the Endocrine System

The endocrine system plays a pivotal role in regulating a wide array of bodily functions through the production and secretion of hormones. It comprises a network of glands that communicate with each other and other organs via hormonal signals to maintain homeostasis, influence growth and development, and manage energy levels, among other critical functions. This chapter will delve into the anatomy of the endocrine system, explore the functions of different hormones and glands, and introduce essential medical terminology relevant to this system. Understanding the endocrine system is fundamental for endocrinologists, general practitioners, and any healthcare provider involved in managing hormonal therapies or treating hormonal imbalances.

Anatomy of the Endocrine System

The endocrine system includes several major glands, each of which produces specific hormones with unique roles:

- **Pituitary Gland**: Often termed the "master gland," it controls other endocrine glands and regulates critical functions such as growth, reproduction, and metabolism.
- **Thyroid Gland**: Produces hormones that regulate the body's metabolic rate, heart and digestive function, muscle control, brain development, and bone maintenance.
- **Adrenal Glands**: Produce hormones that help regulate metabolism, immune system, blood pressure, and response to stress and other essential functions.
- **Pancreas**: Functions as both an endocrine and exocrine gland; it produces insulin, crucial for regulating blood glucose levels.
- **Gonads (Ovaries and Testes)**: Produce sex hormones that influence sexual development and reproductive functions.

Function of the Endocrine System

The endocrine system's primary function is to produce and secrete hormones directly into the bloodstream to be transported to various organs and tissues throughout the body. Hormones are chemical messengers that influence many physiological activities, including:

- **Metabolism and Energy Balance**
- **Growth and Development**
- **Sexual Function and Reproductive Processes**
- **Mood and Stress Management**

- **Bone and Muscle Strength**

Medical Terminology in the Endocrine System

A firm grasp of specific endocrine-related medical terminology is essential for effective communication within the healthcare setting. Important terms include:

- **Diabetes Mellitus**: A group of metabolic diseases characterized by high blood sugar levels over a prolonged period due to insulin production issues or function.
- **Hyperthyroidism and Hypothyroidism**: Conditions resulting from overactive and underactive thyroid gland activity, respectively.
- **Cushing's Syndrome**: A disorder that occurs when the body is exposed to high levels of the hormone cortisol for a long time.
- **Addison's Disease**: A disorder in which the adrenal glands produce insufficient steroid hormones.

Common Endocrine Disorders

Several disorders can impact the efficiency of the endocrine system, affecting overall health:

- **Diabetes Mellitus**: Perhaps the most well-known endocrine disorder, affecting glucose regulation in the body.
- **Thyroid Disorders**: Such as hyperthyroidism and hypothyroidism, which affect metabolism, energy, and overall physiological balance.
- **Polycystic Ovary Syndrome (PCOS)**: A hormonal disorder causing enlarged ovaries with small cysts on the outer edges.

The endocrine system's complexity and its integral role in regulating numerous bodily functions necessitate a comprehensive understanding of its components and their interactions. For healthcare providers, mastering the medical terminology associated with this system enhances their ability to diagnose, discuss, and manage conditions related to hormonal imbalances and glandular dysfunctions. As we continue to explore the interconnectedness of body systems in subsequent chapters, the influence of the endocrine system on processes like metabolism, growth, and reproduction will further illustrate the interconnected nature of human physiology. This knowledge is not only vital for specialists like endocrinologists but also for all health professionals who support patients in managing lifelong conditions influenced by hormonal changes.

Comprehensive Exploration of the Urinary System
Introduction to the Urinary System

The urinary system, a crucial component of the human body, is primarily responsible for the removal of waste products and the regulation of electrolyte and fluid balance. This system plays a vital role in maintaining the body's internal environment, ensuring that chemical levels and fluid volumes are kept within narrow limits. This chapter delves into the anatomy of the urinary system, its functions, and the relevant medical terminology. It also explores common urinary conditions that healthcare professionals, particularly urologists and nephrologists, encounter.

Anatomy of the Urinary System

The urinary system consists of the kidneys, ureters, bladder, and urethra. Each of these components plays a specific role in urine production and excretion:

- **Kidneys**: Two bean-shaped organs located below the ribs toward the middle of the back. They filter blood to remove waste and excess substances, producing urine.

- **Ureters**: Narrow tubes that carry urine from the kidneys to the bladder.
- **Bladder**: A hollow organ that stores urine until it is ready to be excreted.
- **Urethra**: The tube through which urine passes from the bladder out of the body.

Function of the Urinary System

The primary functions of the urinary system include:

- **Waste Excretion**: Filters waste products, toxins, and excess substances like urea, drugs, and food additives from the bloodstream.
- **Regulation of Blood Volume and Pressure**: Controls the volume of blood (and thus blood pressure) by adjusting the amount of water excreted in urine.
- **Regulation of Electrolytes**: Maintains the proper balance of electrolytes, such as sodium, potassium, and phosphate, in the bloodstream.
- **pH Balance**: Regulates the pH level of the blood by adjusting the amount of acids and bases excreted in urine.

Medical Terminology in the Urinary System

Understanding the terminology associated with the urinary system is essential for diagnosing and treating related conditions. Key terms include:

- **Nephrology**: The branch of medicine dealing with kidney function and diseases.
- **Cystitis**: Inflammation of the bladder, often due to infection and leading to frequent, painful urination.
- **Renal Failure**: A condition in which the kidneys lose the ability to filter waste effectively from the blood.

- **Urolithiasis (Kidney Stones)**: Solid masses formed in the kidneys from minerals in the urine.

Common Urinary Conditions

Healthcare professionals frequently encounter several urinary conditions that can affect any part of the system:

- **Urinary Tract Infections (UTIs)**: Infections that can occur anywhere along the urinary tract, including the bladder and kidneys.
- **Kidney Stones**: Hard mineral deposits formed inside the kidneys, which can cause severe pain and blood in urine.
- **Incontinence**: The loss of bladder control, leading to the involuntary leakage of urine.
- **Chronic Kidney Disease (CKD)**: The gradual loss of kidney function over time, often due to diabetes or high blood pressure.

The urinary system's ability to efficiently remove waste and maintain fluid and electrolyte balance is critical for overall health. A thorough understanding of this system's structure, function, and common disorders is indispensable for healthcare providers, especially those specializing in urology and nephrology. Mastery of the relevant medical terminology enhances the ability to discuss these conditions accurately, guide treatment Kent plans, and educate patients about their health. As we explore the interconnected nature of body systems in further chapters, the relationship between the urinary system and other systems, such as the cardiovascular and endocrine systems, will highlight the complex and integrated nature of body physiology. This knowledge is crucial for a holistic approach to healthcare and patient management

. . .

Comprehensive Exploration of the Reproductive Systems

Introduction to the Reproductive Systems

The reproductive systems in humans play a critical role in the continuation of species through the process of reproduction. Comprising distinct male and female anatomical structures, these systems are designed not only for the production and nurturing of new life but also for hormonal regulation that affects various aspects of health. This chapter will detail the anatomy of both male and female reproductive systems, explain key physiological processes, and introduce the medical terminology necessary for professionals specializing in gynecology, obstetrics, and urology.

Anatomy of the Reproductive Systems

Male Reproductive System:

- **Testes**: Produce sperm and testosterone, the primary male sex hormone.
- **Epididymis and Vas Deferens**: Transport and store sperm.
- **Prostate and Seminal Vesicles**: Produce fluids that nourish and transport sperm (semen).

Female Reproductive System:

- **Ovaries**: Produce eggs (ova) and hormones including estrogen and progesterone.
- **Fallopian Tubes**: Transport the ova from the ovaries to the uterus.
- **Uterus**: Nurtures the fertilized ovum that develops into a fetus.
- **Vagina**: Serves as the passage from the uterus to the outside of the body.

Function of the Reproductive Systems

The primary functions of the reproductive systems include:

- **Production of Gametes**: Sperm in males and ova in females.
- **Fertilization**: The process by which sperm and ovum combine to form a zygote.
- **Hormone Production**: Essential for the regulation of sexual development, reproductive cycles, and pregnancy.
- **Gestation**: The development of the embryo and fetus during pregnancy (female).
- **Birth and Lactation**: Delivery of the newborn and subsequent feeding (female).

Medical Terminology in the Reproductive Systems

Accurate medical terminology is crucial for diagnosing and treating conditions related to reproductive health. Some key terms include:

- **Endometriosis**: A painful disorder in which tissue similar to the tissue that normally lines the inside of the uterus grows outside the uterus.
- **Prostatitis**: Inflammation of the prostate gland, often causing swelling or pain.
- **Polycystic Ovary Syndrome (PCOS)**: A hormonal disorder causing enlarged ovaries with small cysts on the outer edges.
- **Erectile Dysfunction (ED)**: The inability to get or keep an erection firm enough for sexual intercourse.

Common Reproductive Conditions

Various reproductive conditions can affect the health of individuals:

- **Infertility**: Affects both men and women and is defined as the inability to conceive after one year of unprotected sex.
- **Prostate Enlargement (Benign Prostatic Hyperplasia)**: A common condition as men age, which can interfere with urination.
- **Cervical and Ovarian Cancers**: Significant health concerns that impact women's reproductive organs.

Understanding the reproductive systems' complex structure and functions is essential for healthcare providers specializing in reproductive health. Mastery of the detailed anatomy, physiological processes, and medical terminology discussed in this chapter enables professionals to provide better patient care, from routine health screenings to treating complex reproductive conditions. As we move forward in the textbook, the interaction between the reproductive systems and other body systems, such as the endocrine system, illustrates the interconnectedness of human physiology, emphasizing the holistic nature of healthcare.

Comprehensive Exploration of the Integumentary System

Introduction to the Integumentary System

The integumentary system, consisting of the skin, hair, nails, and various glands, serves as the body's primary barrier against environmental hazards. It plays critical roles in protection, temperature regulation, and sensory perception. This system is not only the largest organ system of the body but also one of the most important in terms of protective functions. This chapter will delve into the detailed anatomy of the integumentary system, explain its multiple functions, and introduce essential medical terminology that healthcare professionals, particularly dermatologists, need to understand and communicate effectively about skin health and diseases.

Anatomy of the Integumentary System

The integumentary system is anatomically detailed with multiple layers and structures:

- **Skin**: The largest organ of the body, consisting of three main layers—the epidermis (outer layer), dermis (middle layer), and hypodermis (innermost layer).
- **Hair**: Grows from follicles located in the dermis, each hair protects from environmental damage and contributes to sensory input.
- **Nails**: Hard keratin plates growing from the epidermis, providing protection for the distal phalanx and the fingertip.
- **Glands**: Including sweat glands for thermoregulation and sebaceous glands for lubricating the skin and hair.

Function of the Integumentary System

The integumentary system has several essential functions:

- **Protection**: Acts as a barrier that protects the body from mechanical impacts, pathogens, and harmful substances.
- **Temperature Regulation**: Regulates body temperature through sweat production and the dilation or constriction of blood vessels in the skin.
- **Sensory Perception**: Contains numerous nerve endings that detect temperature, touch, pressure, and pain.
- **Vitamin D Synthesis**: Initiates the production of vitamin D in the skin through UV radiation exposure.

Medical Terminology in the Integumentary System

Understanding the specific terminology related to the integumentary system is crucial for diagnosing and treating skin-related conditions. Some important terms include:

- **Dermatitis**: Inflammation of the skin that can cause itchiness, redness, and swelling.
- **Melanoma**: A type of skin cancer that arises from the pigment-producing cells known as melanocytes.
- **Psoriasis**: A chronic autoimmune condition that results in the buildup of skin cells, forming scales and itchy, dry patches.
- **Acne**: A skin condition that occurs when hair follicles become plugged with oil and dead skin cells, leading to whiteheads, blackheads, or pimples.

Common Disorders of the Integumentary System

The integumentary system can be afflicted by a variety of disorders that impact its health and functionality:

- **Eczema**: Also known as atopic dermatitis, it is characterized by red, itchy, and inflamed skin.
- **Skin Cancer**: Including basal cell carcinoma, squamous cell carcinoma, and melanoma, often due to genetic factors and UV exposure.
- **Rosacea**: A chronic skin condition that causes redness and visible blood vessels in the face.

The integumentary system is a complex network that plays vital roles in protection, sensation, and homeostasis. A thorough understanding of this system's structure, functions, and associated pathologies is essential for healthcare providers, especially those specializing in dermatology. This knowledge is not only crucial for diagnosing and treating skin diseases but also for advising on preventive care and cosmetic treatments. As we explore further into other body systems, the connection between skin health and overall physiological health underscores the need for an integrated approach in medicine. This foundational knowledge assists in providing comprehensive care that addresses both specific dermatological issues and their broader health implications.

Comprehensive Exploration of the Lymphatic and Immune Systems

Introduction to the Lymphatic and Immune Systems

The lymphatic and immune systems are critical components of the body's defense mechanism against infectious diseases and play essential roles in maintaining fluid balance within the body. These interconnected systems consist of a network of lymphatic vessels, lymph nodes, and various immune organs and cells that work collaboratively to protect the body from pathogens and maintain internal homeostasis. This chapter will provide an in-depth look at the anatomy and function of these systems, explore key medical terminology, and discuss common lymphatic and immune disorders. Understanding these systems is vital for healthcare professionals specializing in immunology, infectious diseases, and overall patient care.

Anatomy of the Lymphatic and Immune Systems

The lymphatic system includes:

- **Lymphatic Vessels**: A network of conduits that carry lymph, a clear fluid that originates from blood plasma, throughout the body.
- **Lymph Nodes**: Small, bean-shaped structures located along the lymphatic vessels that filter lymph and trap pathogens and debris.

- **Thymus and Spleen**: Primary lymphoid organs where immune cells mature and are stored.

The immune system comprises two main parts:

- **Innate Immunity**: The first line of defense, including physical barriers such as skin and mucous membranes, and immune cells like macrophages.
- **Adaptive Immunity**: A more specialized response involving lymphocytes like B cells and T cells that target specific pathogens.

Function of the Lymphatic and Immune Systems

The primary functions of these systems include:

- **Disease Defense**: Identifying and eliminating pathogens such as bacteria, viruses, and fungi.
- **Fluid Balance**: Collecting and returning interstitial fluid from tissues to the bloodstream, helping maintain internal fluid stability.
- **Waste Removal**: Transporting waste products and cellular debris from the tissues to the lymph nodes for filtration.
- **Immune Surveillance**: Recognizing and destroying abnormal cells, such as cancer cells, before they proliferate.

Medical Terminology in the Lymphatic and Immune Systems

Proficiency in medical terminology related to these systems is essential for accurate diagnosis and treatment of related conditions. Key terms include:

- **Lymphedema**: Swelling that generally occurs in one of your arms or legs due to a blockage in the lymphatic system.
- **Autoimmune Disease**: Conditions where the immune system mistakenly attacks the body's own tissues, such as lupus and multiple sclerosis.
- **Immunodeficiency**: Disorders where part of the immune system is absent or not functioning properly, leaving individuals more susceptible to infections.
- **Hypersensitivity**: Excessive reactions by the immune system, such as allergies or asthma.

Common Disorders of the Lymphatic and Immune Systems

These systems can be affected by various disorders that impact health and well-being:

- **Lymphoma**: A type of cancer that originates in the lymphatic system, primarily affecting lymph nodes and other lymph tissues.
- **HIV/AIDS**: A viral infection that progressively deteriorates the immune system, leading to severe immunodeficiency.
- **Rheumatoid Arthritis**: An autoimmune disorder that primarily affects the joints but can also impact other systems.

The lymphatic and immune systems are fundamental to maintaining health and protecting against disease. Understanding the complexities of these systems allows healthcare professionals to better manage conditions that compromise immune and lymphatic function. Knowledge of these systems is crucial not only for immunologists and infectious disease specialists but also for all healthcare providers due to the widespread impact of immune-related health issues. As we continue to explore the interconnected nature of bodily systems, the role of the lymphatic and immune systems in overall health underscores the importance of an integrated approach to patient care, highlighting the necessity of maintaining immune health in preventing and treating diseases.

As we conclude our extensive exploration of the body systems in Chapter 2, it becomes evident that each system, while distinct in its structure and function, plays an integral role in maintaining the overall health and functionality of the human body. The skeletal system provides the framework, the muscular system facilitates movement, the cardiovascular system ensures nutrient and oxygen distribution, the respiratory system manages gas exchange, and the digestive system processes nutrients. Meanwhile, the urinary system eliminates wastes, the reproductive system perpetuates genetic legacy, the nervous system coordinates both voluntary and involuntary activities, and the endocrine system subtly orchestrates bodily functions through hormonal signals. The integumentary system protects against external threats, and the lymphatic and immune systems defend against internal threats.

This comprehensive understanding is crucial for healthcare professionals across various specialties. By mastering the specific medical terminology associated with each system, they enhance their diagnostic and treatment capabilities. This knowledge enables them to provide superior patient care and engage in more meaningful discussions and collaborations within the scientific and medical communities. It empowers them to handle complex clinical situations with greater confidence and precision, ultimately contributing to improved patient outcomes and advancements in medical science.

Building upon the foundational knowledge of body systems explored in Chapter 2, Chapter 3 will shift focus towards the practical applications in medicine—specifically, diagnostic procedures and pharmacology. This next chapter aims to bridge the gap between theoretical knowledge of bodily functions and the clinical techniques used to assess, diagnose, and treat various medical conditions.

In this chapter, we will delve into a variety of diagnostic tools and methodologies—from imaging techniques like X-rays and MRIs to blood tests and genetic screening—that help clinicians detect and monitor diseases. Understanding these tools is essential for effectively pinpointing health issues within the different body systems discussed previously.

Additionally, we will explore the field of pharmacology, which examines how drugs interact with the body to treat conditions, relieve symptoms, and prevent disease. This section will cover the mechanisms of drug action, the therapeutic uses of different drug classes, and the side effects and potential interactions of medications. As we discuss pharmacology, we will also touch on the importance of personalized medicine and how understanding an individual's unique biological makeup can guide more effective treatment plans.

Chapter 3 promises to provide a comprehensive overview of the crucial tools and knowledge that healthcare professionals utilize to apply their understanding of the body systems in clinical settings. This will not only enhance their ability to treat diseases but also improve their capacity to prevent them, ensuring better health outcomes for patients across all demographics.

Introduction to Chapter 3: Diagnostic Procedures and Pharmacology

Overview of Chapter 3

Chapter 3 of our exploration into medical terminology and applications transitions from the anatomical and physiological complexities of body systems to the practical and clinical tools essential for evaluating and managing patient health. This chapter delves into the realm of diagnostic procedures and pharmacology, areas that are pivotal in the detection, diagnosis, and treatment of diseases. Diagnostic tools and pharmacological therapies are the cornerstones of modern medicine, enabling healthcare professionals to apply their foundational knowledge effectively to achieve optimal patient outcomes.

Comprehensive Exploration of Diagnostic Procedures

Introduction to Diagnostic Procedures

The ability to accurately diagnose diseases is foundational to effective medical treatment and a critical skill for healthcare professionals. This section will provide a detailed overview of the diagnostic procedures that are integral to modern medicine. From conducting physical assessments to utilizing advanced technological tools, this chapter aims to equip students and professionals with the knowledge needed to effectively utilize various diagnostic methods. Understanding and applying these procedures correctly is essential for accurate diagnosis, which in turn guides effective treatment plans.

Physical Assessments

Physical assessments form the cornerstone of the initial diagnostic process in clinical practice. These techniques, executed by skilled healthcare providers, offer a primary means of evaluating a patient's health status and can reveal important information that might not be immediately evident through patient history alone. This section will delve into the specifics of four fundamental physical assessment techniques: auscultation, palpation, inspection, and percussion. Each technique serves a unique purpose and, when combined, they provide a comprehensive overview of a patient's physiological condition, guiding further diagnostic testing and interventions.

Auscultation

Auscultation involves the use of a stethoscope to listen to sounds produced within the body. This non-invasive method is vital for assessing the functioning of the heart, lungs, and other organs:

- **Heart**: Auscultation of the heart includes listening for the rate, rhythm, and character of heartbeats. Abnormal heart sounds, such as murmurs or gallops, can indicate conditions like valve abnormalities or heart failure.
- **Lungs**: By auscultating the lungs, healthcare providers can detect normal and abnormal respiratory sounds. Normal breath sounds vary by location on the chest but typically include vesicular, bronchial, and bronchovesicular sounds. Abnormal sounds, such as wheezing (suggestive of asthma), crackles (indicative of pneumonia or heart failure), and stridor (pointing to airway obstruction), can help pinpoint respiratory issues.
- **Abdomen**: Listening to bowel sounds can provide information on the motility of the gastrointestinal tract. The absence or hyperactivity of these sounds can indicate various gastrointestinal conditions.

Palpation

Palpation is a tactile method where the clinician uses their hands to feel body parts to assess their size, shape, firmness, or location. It is crucial for detecting the characteristics of the skin, underlying structures, and deeper organs:

- **Surface Palpation**: Used to assess the texture, temperature, moisture, and presence of lumps or masses under the skin.
- **Deep Palpation**: Allows the examination of organs like the liver, spleen, and kidneys to assess their size, shape, and any abnormal growths or pain. For example, an enlarged liver can suggest liver disease or heart failure, while tenderness might indicate inflammation or infection.

Inspection

Inspection is the visual examination of the body. It involves looking at the physical appearance, movements, and behavior of the patient, providing clues about their health status:

- **General Appearance**: Observing overall physical condition, hygiene, level of distress, and body habitus.
- **Skin**: Checking for rashes, lesions, bruises, or abnormal pigmentation. Changes in skin appearance can be early indicators of systemic conditions such as jaundice in liver disease or cyanosis in hypoxia.
- **Symmetry**: Observing for asymmetry which might suggest pathologies such as stroke or muscle atrophy.

Percussion

Percussion involves tapping on the body's surface to produce sounds that provide information about the underlying structures. This technique can help determine whether a structure is fluid-filled, solid, or gaseous:

- **Tympany**: Typically heard over air-filled structures, such as the stomach or intestines.
- **Dullness**: Indicates denser organs such as the liver or spleen. Increased dullness can be found in conditions like pleural effusion or enlarged organs.
- **Resonance**: Normal lung sounds during percussion; decreased resonance might suggest pneumonia or other pathologies involving lung consolidation.

Physical assessments are essential skills for healthcare providers, offering crucial data that inform further diagnostic decisions and treatment strategies. Mastery of these techniques requires thorough understanding and significant clinical practice to enhance diagnostic accuracy and patient care. As we progress through this textbook, the integration of these basic diagnostic techniques with advanced tools and detailed knowledge of body systems will underscore the comprehensive approach needed in modern medical practice.

Laboratory Tests

Laboratory testing is an indispensable part of medical diagnostics, providing critical insights that guide clinical decision-making. By analyzing samples of blood, urine, and other bodily fluids, lab tests deliver objective, quantitative data that help confirm clinical suspicions, identify new health issues, and monitor ongoing conditions. This section delves into some of the most fundamental and widely utilized laboratory tests in medicine: the Complete Blood Count (CBC), Metabolic Panel, and Urinalysis. Each test offers specific insights into various aspects of health and plays a crucial role in the diagnostic process.

Complete Blood Count (CBC)

The Complete Blood Count is one of the most common laboratory tests and serves as a broad screening tool for a variety of disorders:

- **Red Blood Cells (RBCs)**: RBC count helps assess the oxygen-carrying capacity of the blood; abnormalities can indicate anemia or polycythemia.
- **White Blood Cells (WBCs)**: WBC count is crucial for evaluating the body's immune response. High levels may indicate an infection or leukemia, while low levels may suggest an immune deficiency.
- **Hemoglobin and Hematocrit**: These tests measure the amount of hemoglobin in the blood and the proportion of blood volume that is made up of red blood cells, respectively, providing information about the blood's ability to carry oxygen.
- **Platelets**: Platelet counts are important for assessing clotting capability; abnormalities can lead to excessive bleeding or clotting disorders.

Metabolic Panel

The Metabolic Panel is another critical test that measures various chemicals in the blood, providing information about the status of the patient's metabolism:

- **Basic Metabolic Panel (BMP)**: Includes tests for blood glucose, calcium, and electrolytes like sodium, potassium, bicarbonate, and chloride, which are vital for cellular function and fluid balance.
- **Comprehensive Metabolic Panel (CMP)**: Includes all the tests in a BMP plus additional tests for proteins and liver enzymes. These measurements can help evaluate liver function, protein levels, and kidney function.

Urinalysis

Urinalysis is a simple yet informative test that analyzes the content of urine. It is frequently used to diagnose urinary tract infections, kidney disease, diabetes, and more:

- **Physical Examination**: Color and clarity can indicate the presence of blood, bile, or other substances.
- **Chemical Examination**: Uses a dipstick test that can detect abnormalities such as high levels of glucose, ketones, proteins, and bilirubin.
- **Microscopic Examination**: Looks for cells, bacterial presence, crystals, or casts that are not normally found in urine.

Importance of Laboratory Tests in Clinical Practice

Laboratory tests are critical in the diagnosis and management of a wide range of diseases. They can:

- **Confirm Diagnosis**: Lab tests can confirm or rule out conditions suspected based on physical examination and patient history.
- **Guide Treatment**: Results can help tailor treatment plans, such as adjusting medication dosages or changing dietary recommendations.
- **Monitor Disease Progression**: Regular testing can track the progress of a disease or the effectiveness of treatment, allowing adjustments as necessary.

Laboratory testing is a vital aspect of modern medicine that significantly enhances diagnostic accuracy and patient care. By providing detailed data about the patient's health, laboratory tests help narrow down potential causes of symptoms, confirm diagnoses, and guide treatment decisions. Understanding the purpose, method, and implications of key laboratory tests like CBC, Metabolic Panels, and Urinalysis is essential for healthcare professionals to effectively interpret results and make informed clinical decisions. This knowledge not only supports acute medical care but also aids in the long-term management of chronic conditions, thereby improving overall patient outcomes. As we continue to explore other diagnostic tools in this chapter, the integration of laboratory testing with other diagnostic modalities will underscore its indispensable role in comprehensive patient assessment and care.

Genetic Testing

Genetic testing comprises a range of sophisticated diagnostic tools that examine an individual's DNA to identify genetic differences or mutations that may influence their health. Unlike conventional diagnostics that detect diseases based on symptoms and physical manifestations, genetic testing can uncover predispositions to illnesses before symptoms arise, offer insights into inherited traits, and assist in crafting personalized treatment strategies. This section delves into three critical areas of genetic testing: Predictive Testing, Carrier Testing, and Pharmacogenomics.

Predictive Testing

Predictive genetic testing is used to detect gene mutations associated with conditions that may appear later in life. This type of testing is particularly valuable for individuals with a family history of certain genetic disorders:

- **Cancer Screening**: Tests like those for BRCA1 or BRCA2 genes can indicate heightened risks for breast and ovarian cancers, allowing individuals to make informed decisions about preventive measures.
- **Neurological Disorders**: Genetic markers linked to diseases such as Huntington's disease or Alzheimer's disease can be identified, providing crucial information for life planning and management.
- **Heart Disease**: Genetic tests can reveal mutations associated with conditions like hypertrophic cardiomyopathy, potentially guiding interventions to mitigate health risks.

Carrier Testing

Carrier testing is crucial for individuals or couples planning to start a family, as it helps determine whether they carry gene mutations that could be passed on to their children:

- **Cystic Fibrosis**: Often screened in carrier testing, this condition requires two copies of a defective gene for the disease to manifest. Knowing carrier status can inform reproductive decisions.
- **Sickle Cell Anemia**: Carrier testing for this disease,

which affects hemoglobin in blood cells, is vital in populations where the disease is prevalent.

- **Tay-Sachs Disease**: Particularly among people of Ashkenazi Jewish descent, carrier testing for Tay-Sachs can prevent the birth of affected offspring, as the disease leads to severe neurological issues.

Pharmacogenomics

Pharmacogenomics combines the fields of pharmacology and genomics to understand how an individual's genetic makeup affects their response to drugs. This approach aims to optimize drug efficacy and minimize side effects:

- **Drug Efficacy**: Genetic variations can affect how well a drug works in an individual's body. For example, certain genetic markers can predict how a patient will metabolize medications used for blood thinning or cholesterol management.
- **Side Effects**: Genetic testing can help predict adverse reactions to drugs, such as severe cutaneous adverse reactions (SCARs) to certain antibiotics or anti-epileptic drugs.
- **Dosage Requirements**: Genetics can dictate the doses needed to achieve therapeutic effects, enhancing treatment safety and effectiveness.

Importance of Genetic Testing in Clinical Practice

Genetic testing represents a transformative shift in modern medicine, offering profound benefits:

- **Risk Assessment**: Provides individuals with the chance to understand their genetic risks and take proactive health measures.

- **Informed Decision-Making**: Empowers individuals and families with genetic information that can guide personal and reproductive decisions.
- **Personalized Medicine**: Facilitates the development of personalized treatment plans that are more effective and have fewer side effects, improving patient care and outcomes.

Genetic testing is a critical component of contemporary diagnostic procedures, offering unparalleled insights into an individual's genetic predispositions and how these may affect their health. By understanding and utilizing genetic information, healthcare professionals can predict disease risks, identify carriers of inheritable diseases, and customize treatments to optimize care. As we progress into a future where medicine becomes increasingly personalized, genetic testing will play an even more pivotal role in guiding healthcare decisions and treatments, marking a significant advancement in our ability to manage and prevent disease effectively.

The Role of Diagnostic Procedures in Medical Practice

Diagnostic procedures are critical tools in the arsenal of healthcare providers. They enable the identification of diseases at an early stage, which can significantly increase the effectiveness of treatment and improve patient outcomes. Additionally, diagnostic testing plays a pivotal role in monitoring the progression of a disease and evaluating the effectiveness of treatment, thereby guiding adjustments in therapy that may be necessary over time.

The section on diagnostic procedures provides a comprehensive understanding of the essential techniques and technologies that underpin effective medical diagnostics. Mastery of these procedures, combined with an understanding of their appropriate application and interpretation, is crucial for any healthcare professional. This knowledge not only enhances the capability to diagnose and treat diseases accurately but also significantly contributes to the advancement of personalized medicine, ultimately leading to better patient care and health outcomes. As we move forward into the next sections, the focus will shift from diagnosis to the treatment modalities that are informed by these diagnostic insights, particularly pharmacology and its applications in medical practice.

Comprehensive Exploration of Imaging Techniques
Introduction to Imaging in Medical Diagnostics

Imaging techniques are crucial in modern medicine for providing a clear visual representation of the internal state of the body. They allow clinicians to detect, diagnose, and monitor diseases or injuries that are not apparent through physical examinations alone. By offering different perspectives and levels of detail, imaging technologies help uncover hidden abnormalities and are indispensable in treatment planning and surgical interventions. This section will delve into the most commonly used imaging modalities, including X-rays, Computed Tomography (CT) scans, Magnetic Resonance Imaging (MRI), and Ultrasound, discussing their specific applications, benefits, and limitations.

X-rays

X-ray imaging is one of the oldest and most commonly used diagnostic tools in medical practice. Utilizing electromagnetic radiation, X-rays can pass through the body to create images that reveal the internal structure of various tissues, especially bones and dense materials. This section will provide an in-depth look at how X-rays work, their primary applications in medical diagnostics, and the limitations and precautions associated with their use.

How X-rays Work

X-rays are a form of electromagnetic radiation with the ability to penetrate different materials, including body tissues. When X-rays pass through the body, they are absorbed in varying degrees by different tissues based on their density:

- **Dense Materials**: Such as bones, absorb more X-rays and appear white on the resulting images.
- **Soft Tissues**: Such as muscles and fat, absorb fewer X-rays and appear in shades of gray.

A detector on the opposite side of the body from the X-ray source captures the rays after they pass through and creates an image based on the varying levels of absorption—providing critical visual data about the body's internal structures.

Applications of X-ray Imaging

X-ray imaging has broad applications in medicine, ranging from routine screening to complex diagnostics. Key applications include:

- **Bone Imaging**: X-rays are fundamental in orthopedics for diagnosing broken bones, joint dislocations, and other skeletal abnormalities. The high contrast of X-rays makes them ideal for visualizing the integrity of the bone structure.
- **Chest Imaging**: In pulmonology, X-rays are used to assess the lungs and heart. They can identify lung conditions such as pneumonia, lung cancer, and pulmonary edema, as well as some heart-related issues like an enlarged cardiac silhouette suggesting heart failure.
- **Dental Imaging**: Dentists use X-rays to view the teeth and jawbone, helping to identify cavities, tooth decay, and impacted teeth.
- **Abdominal Imaging**: Used less frequently for soft tissues, X-rays can still help in diagnosing conditions involving dense structures in the abdomen, such as kidney stones or certain types of gallstones.

Limitations and Risks of X-rays

Despite their widespread utility, X-rays are not without limitations and potential risks:

- **Radiation Exposure**: X-rays involve exposure to ionizing radiation, which can pose a risk of developing cancer after repeated exposure. The risk is generally low but must be managed carefully, particularly in children and pregnant women.
- **Limited Detail in Soft Tissues**: X-rays are less effective for viewing soft tissues compared to other imaging modalities like MRI or ultrasound. Soft tissues often require contrast agents or different imaging techniques for detailed examination.

X-ray imaging remains a cornerstone of diagnostic imaging in medicine due to its availability, speed, and effectiveness in visualizing dense tissues like bones. While there are inherent limitations and risks, the benefits of X-ray imaging often outweigh these concerns, particularly in acute care settings where quick diagnosis is critical. Understanding the principles, applications, and safety considerations of X-ray imaging is essential for healthcare professionals to utilize this technology effectively and responsibly. As we continue to explore other imaging techniques, the role of X-rays as a foundational imaging tool in the broader context of medical diagnostics becomes even clearer, underscoring its indispensable value in modern healthcare.

Computed Tomography (CT) Scans

Computed Tomography (CT) scans represent a significant advancement in diagnostic imaging technology. Utilizing X-rays, CT scans produce cross-sectional images of the body, offering a more detailed look at internal structures than traditional X-rays. This section will delve into how CT scans work, their primary applications in medical diagnostics, and the considerations associated with their use, including risks and limitations.

How CT Scans Work

CT scans enhance the utility of traditional X-rays by taking multiple images from different angles and using computer processing to create cross-sectional views of the body's internal structures. This process involves:

- **X-ray Emission**: A rotating X-ray beam circles around the part of the body being examined, capturing numerous images from various angles.
- **Image Reconstruction**: The X-ray information is sent to a computer that reconstructs the data into two-dimensional slice images of the body, which can be further assembled to create 3D models for in-depth analysis.

Applications of CT Scans

CT scans are invaluable in various medical fields due to their ability to provide detailed images of soft tissues, bones, and blood vessels:

- **Detailed Visualization**: CT scans excel in identifying complex bone fractures, visualizing tumors, and detecting abnormalities in organs. They are crucial in emergency settings for assessing internal injuries and in oncology for pinpointing the location and stage of cancers.
- **Contrast Use**: For enhanced detail, a contrast agent can be injected into the bloodstream, which helps to delineate blood vessels and highlight areas of the body that might be difficult to see, such as inflammatory processes or particular types of tumors.

- **Heart Disease Diagnosis**: CT angiography, which involves the use of contrast material, is particularly effective for examining the coronary arteries and diagnosing heart disease.

Limitations and Risks of CT Scans

While CT scans are a powerful diagnostic tool, they come with several risks and limitations that must be carefully considered:

- **Higher Radiation Doses**: CT scans involve higher levels of ionizing radiation compared to standard X-rays. The cumulative effect of multiple scans over time can increase the risk of cancer, making risk-benefit analysis crucial, especially in non-emergency scenarios.
- **Contrast-Induced Reactions**: The use of contrast dyes, while helpful for enhancing image quality, can lead to allergic reactions in some patients. These reactions range from mild (such as a rash) to severe (such as anaphylactic shock), depending on the individual's sensitivity to the contrast material.
- **Cost and Accessibility**: CT scans are typically more expensive and less available than standard X-rays, which can be limiting factors in certain healthcare settings.

CT scans are a cornerstone of modern medical imaging, providing detailed insights that are critical for diagnosing a wide range of conditions, from acute traumatic injuries to complex diseases like cancer and heart disease. Understanding how to effectively use and interpret CT scans, while managing the associated risks, is essential for healthcare professionals across multiple specialties. This knowledge not only aids in the accurate diagnosis and management of patient conditions but also enhances the ability to conduct thorough medical research and develop more advanced diagnostic and treatment proto-cols. As imaging technology continues to evolve, CT scans remain integral in the broader context of medical diagnostics, combining high-resolution imaging capabilities with rapid data processing to support superior patient care.

Magnetic Resonance Imaging (MRI)

Magnetic Resonance Imaging (MRI) is a sophisticated diagnostic tool that utilizes powerful magnets and radio waves to generate detailed images of the organs and tissues within the body. Unlike X-rays and CT scans, MRI does not rely on ionizing radiation, making it a safer option for repeated imaging. This section will explore how MRI works, its primary applications, and the challenges and limitations associated with its use in clinical settings.

How MRI Works

MRI machines use a strong magnetic field and radio waves to manipulate the natural magnetic properties of hydrogen atoms in the body:

- **Magnetic Field**: When a patient enters the MRI scanner, a powerful magnetic field temporarily realigns water molecules in the body.
- **Radio Waves**: The machine emits a radio frequency pulse that specifically targets these aligned hydrogen atoms, causing them to produce faint signals.
- **Signal Detection and Image Formation**: These signals are detected by the scanner and analyzed by a computer to create detailed cross-sectional images of the body, which can be compiled to form three-dimensional images for thorough examination.

Applications of MRI

MRI is renowned for its exceptional ability to produce high-resolution images of soft tissues, making it an indispensable tool in various medical specialties:

- **Soft Tissue Imaging**: MRI's capability to visualize soft tissues is unmatched. It is particularly effective for assessing conditions involving the brain, spinal cord, nerves, muscles, ligaments, and tendons. This makes it invaluable for diagnosing a broad range of neurological conditions, musculoskeletal disorders, and soft tissue injuries.
- **Functional MRI (fMRI)**: This advanced MRI technique measures and maps the brain's activity by detecting changes associated with blood flow. When an area of the brain is more active, it consumes more oxygen and blood flow to that region increases. The fMRI can detect these changes, providing insights into brain function and enhancing our understanding of brain organization and neural connectivity.

Limitations and Challenges of MRI

While MRI is a powerful imaging tool, it comes with several limitations that can affect its use:

- **High Cost**: MRI scans are significantly more expensive than other imaging modalities, such as X-rays and CT scans. This can limit accessibility for some patients and healthcare systems.
- **Long Scan Times**: MRI scans can take anywhere from 15 minutes to over an hour, depending on the details required. The need for patients to remain still during the scan to avoid blurring the images can be challenging, especially for those who are claustrophobic or uncomfortable in enclosed spaces.

- **Constraints with Metal Implants**: Due to the use of strong magnetic fields, MRI is not suitable for patients with certain types of metal implants, such as some pacemakers, cochlear implants, and certain types of clips used in brain surgeries.

Magnetic Resonance Imaging (MRI) is a revolutionary tool in medical diagnostics, offering detailed images without the risks associated with ionizing radiation. Its ability to provide precise, high-resolution images of soft tissues makes it critical for diagnosing a wide array of medical conditions. However, the effectiveness of MRI must be balanced against its higher costs, longer procedure times, and limitations with certain patients. As technology advances and becomes more integrated into medical practice, the potential applications of MRI and its variants like fMRI continue to expand, promising even greater contributions to medical science and patient care. Understanding the capabilities and limitations of MRI is essential for healthcare professionals to utilize this technology effectively and responsibly in their clinical practice.

Ultrasound

Ultrasound imaging, or sonography, is a versatile and widely used diagnostic tool that employs high-frequency sound waves to create real-time images of the internal structures of the body. Unlike other imaging modalities that rely on radiation, ultrasound uses sound waves, making it one of the safest methods for internal visualization. This section will explore how ultrasound works, its primary applications in medicine, and the factors that influence its effectiveness.

How Ultrasound Works

Ultrasound imaging involves the following steps:

- **Transducer Probe**: This device emits high-frequency sound waves that are directed into the body tissues. The probe also receives the echoes of these sound waves as they bounce back from different tissues.
- **Sound Wave Transmission and Echo Detection**: As the sound waves travel through the body, they encounter tissues of varying densities. Each type of tissue reflects these sound waves back to the probe at different speeds and intensities.
- **Image Formation**: The ultrasound machine interprets these echoes and uses them to create an image that is displayed on a monitor. These images can show movement, enabling real-time visualization of bodily functions.

Applications of Ultrasound Imaging

Ultrasound is indispensable in several medical fields due to its safety and efficacy:

- **Pregnancy**: Ultrasound is crucial in obstetrics where it is used to monitor the development of the fetus, assess the health of the mother, and plan for delivery. It can provide detailed images of the fetus, placenta, and uterus, helping in the assessment of fetal growth, position, and the detection of potential abnormalities.
- **Cardiac Assessments**: In cardiology, echocardiograms (ultrasound scans of the heart) are vital for evaluating heart structure and function. They help in diagnosing heart conditions, assessing damage after a heart attack, and monitoring heart diseases over time.

Advantages of Ultrasound

Ultrasound imaging offers several significant benefits:

- **Safety**: As it does not use ionizing radiation, ultrasound is safe for all ages and stages of life, including during pregnancy.
- **Non-invasive**: With no needles, injections, or incisions required, ultrasound is one of the least invasive imaging techniques available.
- **Real-time Imaging**: Ultrasound provides real-time imaging, making it ideal for guiding minimally invasive procedures such as biopsies or fluid drainage.

Limitations of Ultrasound

Despite its advantages, ultrasound imaging does have limitations:

- **Image Quality**: The quality of ultrasound images can be significantly affected by the patient's body type; for instance, the sound waves can be impeded by dense bone or are absorbed by fatty tissue, which can obscure clear imaging.
- **Operator Dependency**: The accuracy of an ultrasound examination can greatly depend on the skill and experience of the technician or physician operating the device. Proper interpretation of ultrasound images requires significant expertise.

Ultrasound imaging is a fundamental tool in diagnostic medicine, valued for its safety, cost-effectiveness, and dynamic imaging capabilities. It is particularly renowned for its applications in prenatal care and cardiac assessments but is versatile enough to be used in many other areas of medicine as well. Understanding the principles of ultrasound, its applications, and limitations is essential for healthcare professionals to utilize this technology effectively, ensuring optimal patient outcomes. As ultrasound technology continues to evolve, its applications in medical diagnostics and treatment are expected to expand, further underscoring its critical role in modern healthcare practices.

Each imaging modality has its specific applications and plays a pivotal role in the comprehensive evaluation of health conditions. Understanding these tools, their appropriate uses, and their limitations is crucial for all healthcare professionals, particularly those involved in diagnostics, emergency medicine, and specialized fields such as oncology and cardiology. As we move forward, a deeper understanding of these imaging techniques, coupled with advancements in technology, will continue to enhance diagnostic accuracy and improve patient outcomes. The ability to effectively communicate these imaging results is also essential, requiring familiarity with the specialized terminology associated with each technique. This foundation prepares us to explore pharmacology and treatment strategies in subsequent sections, where these diagnostic insights are translated into clinical actions.

Comprehensive Exploration of Pharmacology
Introduction to Pharmacology

Pharmacology is the branch of medicine that focuses on the study of drugs and their interactions with the living systems. It involves understanding how drugs work, their side effects, their absorption and distribution, metabolism, and excretion. This knowledge is crucial for the development, testing, and clinical use of medications aimed at improving patient outcomes. This section of the chapter will cover the fundamental aspects of pharmacology, including drug classifications, pharmacodynamics, pharmacokinetics, and the drug development and approval process.

Drug Classifications

Understanding the classification of drugs is fundamental for healthcare providers, enabling them to prescribe the most effective and appropriate medication for various medical conditions. Drug classifications help organize medications into different groups based on their therapeutic use or mechanism of action, simplifying the complex landscape of available treatments. This section will delve into the key categories of drugs, including antibiotics, antihypertensives, and antidepressants, providing insights into their uses, mechanisms, and examples.

Antibiotics

Antibiotics are agents specifically designed to combat bacterial infections. They either kill bacteria or prevent them from reproducing and growing, thus aiding the immune system in eliminating the pathogen. Understanding the different classes of antibiotics is crucial due to the varying resistance patterns and infection types they target:

- **Penicillins** (e.g., amoxicillin, penicillin V): Work by interfering with the bacterial cell wall synthesis, which is essential for bacteria's survival and growth.
- **Cephalosporins** (e.g., cefdinir, cephalexin): Similar to penicillins but with a broader spectrum of activity and resistance to beta-lactamase enzymes produced by some bacteria.
- **Fluoroquinolones** (e.g., ciprofloxacin, levofloxacin): Act by inhibiting bacterial DNA synthesis, effective against a wide range of infections including urinary tract, respiratory, and skin infections.
- **Macrolides** (e.g., erythromycin, azithromycin): Inhibit protein synthesis within bacterial cells and are particularly useful against respiratory infections and sexually transmitted diseases.

Antihypertensives

Antihypertensives are medications used to lower high blood pressure, a major risk factor for cardiovascular diseases. Effective management of hypertension involves different classes of drugs, each working through a different mechanism:

- **Beta-blockers** (e.g., propranolol, metoprolol): Reduce blood pressure by slowing down the heart rate and decreasing the heart's output of blood.
- **ACE inhibitors** (e.g., lisinopril, enalapril): Block the production of a hormone that narrows blood vessels, thereby relaxing the vessels and reducing blood pressure.
- **Diuretics** (e.g., furosemide, hydrochlorothiazide): Help eliminate excess salt and water from the body through urine, which helps to lower blood pressure.

Antidepressants

Antidepressants are used to treat various mood disorders, including depression, anxiety, and dysthymia. Their efficacy depends on their ability to alter neurotransmitter levels in the brain, particularly those involved in mood regulation:

- **Selective Serotonin Reuptake Inhibitors (SSRIs)** (e.g., fluoxetine, sertraline): Increase levels of serotonin in the brain by blocking its reabsorption into neurons, leading to improved mood and emotional stability.
- **Tricyclic Antidepressants (TCAs)** (e.g., amitriptyline, nortriptyline): Older class of drugs that work by blocking the reabsorption of serotonin and norepinephrine, but with more potential side effects compared to SSRIs.
- **Monoamine Oxidase Inhibitors (MAOIs)** (e.g., phenelzine, tranylcypromine): Block the monoamine oxidase enzyme that breaks down neurotransmitters in the brain, thus increasing their levels and effects.

. . .

The classification of drugs into categories based on therapeutic use or mechanism of action is essential for healthcare providers in prescribing the right medication. This systematic approach not only aids in the effective treatment of various conditions but also minimizes potential risks and side effects associated with pharmacological therapy. As the field of pharmacology continues to evolve, staying informed about these classifications and their updates is crucial for all medical professionals. This knowledge ensures that patient care is both effective and up-to-date, reflecting the latest advances in medical science and therapeutic practices.

Pharmacodynamics and Pharmacokinetics

Pharmacodynamics and pharmacokinetics are pivotal concepts in pharmacology, each addressing different aspects of how drugs interact with the body. Pharmacodynamics explains the effects drugs have on the body, while pharmacokinetics describes what the body does to the drugs. These areas are crucial for developing effective treatment regimens and understanding how various factors can alter drug efficacy and safety. This section will provide a detailed overview of both concepts, highlighting their roles in clinical practice.

Pharmacodynamics

Pharmacodynamics focuses on the relationship between drug concentration at the site of action and the resulting effect, including the mechanism of action, therapeutic effects, and side effects. Key aspects of pharmacodynamics include:

- **Mechanism of Action**: This refers to how a drug produces its effects in the body. For example, antihypertensive drugs may lower blood pressure by dilating blood vessels or reducing heart rate.

- **Therapeutic Effects**: These are the desired, beneficial effects of a drug intended to alleviate symptoms or cure diseases. Understanding the therapeutic effects helps clinicians to choose the most appropriate medication for a specific condition.
- **Side Effects**: These are unintended, often undesirable effects of a drug. Side effects can vary widely from minor to severe and may affect medication adherence or require treatment modification.
- **Drug Interactions**: Pharmacodynamic interactions can occur when one drug alters the effect of another. For instance, when two drugs that depress the central nervous system (such as alcohol and benzodiazepines) are taken together, they can significantly increase each other's effects, leading to enhanced sedation or even respiratory depression.

Understanding pharmacodynamics is crucial for predicting how drugs will behave in different patients, under various conditions, and in combination with other drugs.

Pharmacokinetics

Pharmacokinetics describes how the body absorbs, distributes, metabolizes, and excretes drugs. This knowledge helps to determine the dosage and frequency of drug administration to achieve optimal therapeutic levels without causing toxicity. The four primary phases of pharmacokinetics are:

- **Absorption**: The process by which a drug enters the bloodstream from its site of administration. Factors such as drug formulation, route of administration, and gastrointestinal motility can influence absorption.
- **Distribution**: Once in the bloodstream, drugs are distributed to tissues and organs. The extent of

distribution depends on blood flow, tissue permeability, and protein binding.

- **Metabolism**: Drugs are metabolized primarily in the liver. Enzymes in the liver modify drugs into metabolites that are often easier for the body to eliminate. Genetic differences in metabolism can lead to varying effects of drugs among individuals.
- **Excretion**: The final phase where drugs and their metabolites are eliminated from the body, primarily through the kidneys. Impaired renal function can lead to drug accumulation and toxicity.

Factors influencing pharmacokinetics include patient-specific variables such as age, body weight, liver function, kidney function, and genetic factors. These can significantly affect how a drug is handled by the body and can require dose adjustments.

Pharmacodynamics and pharmacokinetics are foundational concepts in pharmacology that ensure effective and safe medication use. A thorough understanding of these principles is essential for healthcare providers to optimize drug therapy, minimize side effects, and achieve the best possible outcomes for patients. This knowledge not only helps in prescribing and managing medications but also in educating patients about how drugs work and what to expect during treatment. As we continue to advance in the field of pharmacology, the integration of pharmacodynamic and pharmacokinetic principles with emerging technologies and personalized medicine will further enhance our ability to treat diseases more effectively.

Drug Development and Approval

The journey of bringing a new drug to market is a complex, highly regulated process crucial for ensuring that all pharmaceuticals are both safe and effective. This multi-stage process involves extensive research, testing, and regulatory review, demanding substantial investment of time, resources, and expertise. Understanding each phase of drug development and approval is essential for healthcare professionals, as it influences clinical practices and patient care. This section will detail the key stages involved in drug development, from preclinical testing to regulatory approval.

Preclinical Testing

Preclinical testing marks the initial phase of drug development:

- **Laboratory and Animal Studies**: Before testing new drugs in humans, researchers must first establish preliminary efficacy, toxicity, pharmacokinetic, and pharmacodynamic information in vitro (in laboratory experiments) and in vivo (in animal studies).
- **Safety Profiles**: This stage is critical for identifying potential toxic effects and determining safe dosage levels. These studies help to predict how the drug might interact with the human body and what side effects might occur.
- **Regulatory Review**: Data from these tests are submitted to regulatory authorities, who decide whether the drug is safe enough to move forward to clinical trials.

Clinical Trials

Clinical trials test the drug's safety and efficacy in human subjects and are typically divided into three phases:

- **Phase I**: Conducts initial safety testing in a small group of healthy volunteers or patients, focusing on drug metabolism, pharmacokinetics, and side effects.
- **Phase II**: Involves a larger patient group to assess the drug's effectiveness and further evaluate its safety.
- **Phase III**: Expands this evaluation to even larger groups to confirm effectiveness, monitor side effects, compare it to commonly used treatments, and collect information that will allow the drug to be used safely.

Each phase is designed to answer specific research questions, and progression to the next phase is contingent upon demonstrating safety and efficacy.

Regulatory Approval

After a drug has successfully passed through all phases of clinical trials, it enters the regulatory review process:

- **Submission of a New Drug Application (NDA)**: The drug manufacturer submits all data from preclinical and clinical trials to a regulatory body, such as the U.S. Food and Drug Administration (FDA), requesting the approval to market the drug.
- **Review Process**: Regulatory authorities review the NDA to ensure the drug is safe and effective for its intended use and that the benefits outweigh any risks.
- **Post-Marketing Surveillance**: Once approved, the drug enters the market, but it remains under surveillance to monitor any adverse effects from wider use that were not apparent in clinical trials. This phase may lead to further restrictions or even withdrawal of the drug if necessary.

The drug development and approval process is designed to ensure that all medications available on the market are safe and effective for public use. Understanding this process is vital for healthcare professionals, as it directly impacts the treatment options available and informs clinical decision-making. Additionally, knowledge of this process is crucial for addressing patient queries about new treatments and providing reassurance about the safety and regulatory oversight of the drugs they use. As new technologies and methodologies emerge, the drug development process continues to evolve, potentially speeding up the time it takes to bring effective new treatments to market while maintaining strict safety standards.

Pharmacology is a dynamic field that plays a vital role in the healthcare system by providing tools necessary for the treatment and prevention of disease. A thorough understanding of pharmacology enhances the ability of healthcare professionals to prescribe medications appropriately, manage patient care effectively, and participate in the development of new therapies. As we advance further into the clinical applications in subsequent chapters, the interplay between diagnosis, pharmacological treatment, and patient management will underscore the importance of an integrated approach in healthcare. This comprehensive knowledge not only ensures better patient outcomes but also drives innovation in medical research and therapeutic practices.

Summarizing Diagnostic Procedures and Pharmacology

Chapter 3 has provided an in-depth exploration of the diagnostic procedures and pharmacology essential to modern medical practice. By dissecting the realms of imaging, laboratory tests, genetic testing, and the complexities of pharmacology, this chapter has equipped healthcare professionals with the knowledge necessary to understand and implement these tools effectively.

The comprehensive review of diagnostic tools, from X-rays and MRIs to sophisticated genetic testing, underscores their importance in identifying and understanding patient conditions. These tools not only facilitate early and accurate diagnosis but also help monitor disease progression and response to treatment. In an era where medicine is becoming increasingly personalized, the role of precise and timely diagnosis is more critical than ever.

Pharmacology remains a cornerstone of medical treatment. Understanding drug classifications, pharmacodynamics, and pharmacokinetics is crucial for prescribing appropriate therapies and managing patient care. This knowledge ensures that treatments are not only effective but also safe, minimizing potential side effects and improving patient outcomes.

While the advancements in diagnostic and pharmaceutical sciences offer immense benefits, they also come with challenges and ethical considerations. The use of genetic testing, for instance, raises questions about privacy, consent, and the potential for genetic discrimination. Similarly, the increasing complexity of pharmacological treatments necessitates ongoing education and awareness of drug interactions and contraindications.

As technology and science advance, the field of medical diagnostics and pharmacology will continue to evolve. Innovations in imaging and genetics promise to enhance our capabilities for early disease detection and targeted treatment strategies, moving towards a more preventive and personalized healthcare paradigm.

Healthcare professionals must stay informed and adept at utilizing new tools and technologies as they become available. Continuous professional development and adherence to best practices in diagnostics and pharmacology are essential for providing the highest standard of care.

As we conclude Chapter 3, we pave the way for Chapter 4, which will delve into emerging technologies and future trends in medicine. This upcoming chapter will explore how innovations such as artificial intelligence, telemedicine, and advanced biomedical devices are set to revolutionize healthcare delivery. It will examine how these technologies not only enhance diagnostic and treatment capabilities but also how they reshape the very fabric of medical practice, emphasizing the need for an adaptable, forward-thinking approach in healthcare.

Chapter 4 will continue to build on the foundational knowledge provided in this chapter, demonstrating how to integrate new technologies into clinical practice responsibly and effectively. This progression underscores the dynamic nature of healthcare and the continuous need for professionals to evolve with their field, embracing new challenges and opportunities that ultimately aim to improve patient care and health outcomes.

Chapter 3
Diseases and Conditions

hapter 3, "Diseases and Conditions," serves as a vital segment in the continuum of medical education, shifting focus from the diagnostic tools and pharmacological treatments discussed in previous chapters to a more detailed examination of various diseases and conditions. This chapter aims to deepen healthcare professionals' understanding of common diseases, familiarize them with the terminology used to describe symptoms and signs, and explore the pathology underlying various medical conditions. By integrating this knowledge, healthcare providers will be better equipped to diagnose, manage, and discuss these conditions effectively with both colleagues and patients.

Common Diseases

The first section of this chapter will cover the terminology associated with prevalent diseases affecting the population. This includes a wide array of chronic and acute conditions such as diabetes, hypertension, asthma, and infectious diseases like influenza and COVID-19. Each disease will be discussed in detail, focusing on:

- **Epidemiology**: Understanding the incidence, distribution, and possible control of diseases.
- **Risk Factors**: Identifying who is more likely to develop the disease based on genetic, environmental, and lifestyle factors.
- **Management Strategies**: Overview of current treatments and guidelines for managing these conditions effectively.

Symptoms and Signs

The ability to accurately describe and interpret symptoms and signs is fundamental in medical practice. This section will delve into the vocabulary used to detail how diseases present in patients, including descriptions of pain, fever, inflammation, and other common manifestations of diseases. It will cover:

- **Subjective Symptoms**: Symptoms reported by the patient, such as pain levels, fatigue, and feelings of discomfort.
- **Objective Signs**: Observable signs that can be measured and verified by a healthcare professional, such as rashes, swelling, or abnormal laboratory results.

Pathology

Understanding the pathology of diseases—the study of the causes and effects of these conditions—is crucial for any healthcare professional. This section will explore:

- **Etiology**: The cause or origin of a disease, whether it be genetic, environmental, or infectious.
- **Pathogenesis**: The mechanism through which the disease develops and progresses.
- **Morphology**: The structural changes in cells or tissues caused by disease.

Chapter 4 will not only enhance healthcare professionals' literacy in medical terminology related to diseases and conditions but also deepen their understanding of how these ailments affect human health. This comprehensive approach ensures that professionals are well-prepared to handle the complexities of patient care, from diagnosis through to treatment and management. As the chapter unfolds, readers will gain insights that are critical for effective communication within the healthcare environment and improved patient outcomes.

Comprehensive Exploration of Common Diseases
Introduction to Common Diseases

The study of common diseases encompasses an understanding of the various ailments that significantly impact public health across the globe. This section aims to provide healthcare professionals and students with a detailed examination of prevalent chronic and acute diseases, such as diabetes, hypertension, asthma, influenza, and COVID-19. By exploring the epidemiology, risk factors, and management strategies associated with these diseases, this chapter will equip medical practitioners with the necessary knowledge to diagnose, treat, and manage these conditions effectively.

Epidemiology of Common Diseases

Epidemiology is the study of how often diseases occur in different groups of people and why. Understanding the epidemiology of common diseases is crucial for effective public health planning, disease prevention, and resource allocation. This section aims to provide an in-depth exploration of the epidemiological factors that define the occurrence and spread of prevalent diseases, such as diabetes, hypertension, asthma, influenza, and COVID-19. Each disease presents unique challenges and patterns, which can be understood through a detailed examination of their incidence, prevalence, distribution patterns, and outbreak information.

Incidence and Prevalence

- **Incidence** refers to the number of new cases of a disease that develop in a given period among a specified population. It is crucial for understanding the risk of contracting the disease within a specific timeframe.
- **Prevalence** measures the total number of cases, both new and existing, at a particular point in time within a given population. This helps gauge the overall burden of the disease on society.

For instance, the prevalence of diabetes in a community can illustrate how widespread the disease is, while the incidence can indicate how rapidly new cases are emerging. Both metrics are critical for healthcare planning and determining the allocation of resources for treatment and prevention efforts.

Distribution Patterns

Understanding the distribution of diseases involves examining how they are spread across different regions and among various demographic and socio-economic groups:

- **Geographic Distribution**: Diseases often vary in frequency in different areas due to environmental factors, climate, and local health policies. For example, malaria is primarily concentrated in tropical areas due to the presence of the mosquito vectors that transmit the disease.
- **Demographic Factors**: Age, sex, and ethnicity can significantly influence disease patterns. Osteoporosis is more prevalent in older women, partly due to the effects of menopause on bone density.
- **Socio-economic Factors**: Income levels, access to healthcare, lifestyle choices, and educational attainment can all affect disease prevalence. Conditions like type 2 diabetes and hypertension have higher prevalence rates in populations with higher rates of obesity and sedentary

lifestyles, which are often influenced by socio-economic status.

Outbreak and Pandemic Information

For infectious diseases, understanding the dynamics of outbreaks and pandemics is vital:

- **Outbreak Investigation**: This involves studying the sudden rise in the occurrence of a disease in a specific geographical area or population. Epidemiologists track these increases to identify the source and to control the spread.
- **Pandemic Declaration**: A pandemic occurs when an infectious disease spreads across multiple countries or continents, affecting a large number of people. The criteria for declaring a pandemic involve not only the geographical spread but also the severity and impact of the disease. For example, COVID-19 was declared a pandemic due to its widespread transmission globally coupled with sustained person-to-person spread.

Epidemiology provides a framework for understanding the complex dynamics of disease transmission and prevalence in populations. By studying the incidence, prevalence, and distribution patterns of diseases, public health officials and healthcare providers can develop targeted strategies to prevent and manage health problems more effectively. This understanding is also essential for predicting future trends in disease spread and impact, which is crucial for preparing public health interventions and allocating resources where they are most needed. As students and healthcare professionals delve into the epidemiology of common diseases, they equip themselves with the knowledge necessary to contribute to broader public health efforts, aiming to reduce the incidence and impact of these diseases globally.

Risk Factors for Common Diseases

Understanding the risk factors associated with common diseases is essential for predicting susceptibility, implementing preventive measures, and tailoring treatment strategies. This section aims to provide a comprehensive overview of the various factors that contribute to the development of prevalent health conditions such as diabetes, hypertension, asthma, and more. By examining genetic, environmental, and lifestyle factors, healthcare professionals and students can gain insights into the complex interactions that predispose individuals to these diseases.

Genetic Factors

- **Role of Genetics**: Genetics play a crucial role in the development of many diseases. Certain genes can increase an individual's risk of developing specific conditions. For example:
- **Diabetes**: Genetic predisposition affects the body's ability to produce or respond to insulin, significantly influencing the risk of developing type 2 diabetes.
- **Hypertension**: Several genes are associated with blood pressure regulation, and variations in these genes can lead to an increased risk of hypertension.

Understanding these genetic factors can help in identifying individuals at higher risk and potentially guide preventive and therapeutic strategies based on genetic screening.

Environmental Influences

- **Impact of the Environment**: Environmental factors can significantly influence the onset and progression of diseases. Key environmental influences include:

- **Pollution**: Exposure to air pollutants is a major risk factor for respiratory diseases such as asthma. Pollutants can trigger inflammation in the airways, leading to asthma attacks.
- **Workplace Hazards**: Certain occupations expose individuals to specific risks, such as asbestos exposure increasing the risk of mesothelioma, a type of lung cancer.

Addressing these environmental risk factors often requires public health interventions and regulations to reduce exposure and protect at-risk populations.

Lifestyle Choices

- **Influence of Lifestyle**: Lifestyle choices are among the most significant modifiable risk factors for numerous diseases. Important lifestyle factors include:
- **Diet**: Unhealthy eating habits can lead to obesity, diabetes, and heart diseases. Diets high in saturated fats, sugars, and salt are particularly detrimental.
- **Physical Activity**: Sedentary lifestyles increase the risk of numerous conditions, including cardiovascular diseases and diabetes. Regular physical activity can mitigate these risks by improving cardiovascular health and metabolic function.
- **Smoking and Alcohol Consumption**: Smoking is a major risk factor for lung diseases and cancers, while excessive alcohol consumption can lead to liver diseases and increase the risk of hypertension.

Promoting healthy lifestyle choices through education and

community programs is crucial for preventing many common diseases.

The study of risk factors for common diseases is pivotal in preventive medicine. By understanding how genetic predispositions, environmental exposures, and lifestyle choices contribute to disease development, healthcare professionals can advise patients on how to reduce their risks and potentially prevent certain conditions. Moreover, this knowledge is essential for developing public health policies and interventions aimed at reducing the prevalence and impact of these diseases on a societal level. As we continue to explore the pathology and symptoms of common diseases, integrating our understanding of risk factors will enhance our ability to manage and prevent these conditions effectively.

Management Strategies for Common Diseases

Effective management of common diseases is crucial not only for improving patient outcomes but also for enhancing overall quality of life. This section provides a detailed overview of the various strategies employed to manage prevalent chronic and infectious diseases such as diabetes, hypertension, asthma, and more. By outlining medical treatments, lifestyle modifications, and preventive measures, this guide aims to equip healthcare professionals with the tools needed to support their patients in managing these conditions effectively.

Medical Treatments

Medical treatments are often the first line of defense in managing diseases and typically involve pharmacological interventions tailored to each specific condition:

- **Diabetes**: Management typically involves insulin therapy for Type 1 diabetes, and for Type 2, a combination of oral hypoglycemics like metformin, and sometimes insulin, depending on the severity and progression of the disease.

- **Hypertension**: Includes a range of antihypertensive medications such as ACE inhibitors, beta-blockers, diuretics, and calcium channel blockers, which work in different ways to lower blood pressure.
- **Asthma**: Managed through inhaled corticosteroids to reduce inflammation and bronchodilators to relieve symptoms during asthma attacks.

Each medication regimen must be carefully chosen based on the individual patient's health profile, disease severity, and response to previous treatments, ensuring the most effective and least disruptive therapy is applied.

Lifestyle Modifications

Lifestyle modifications play a critical role in managing chronic diseases, often in conjunction with medical treatments:

- **Diet**: Nutritional counseling is essential, for example, reducing sugar intake in diabetes, lowering salt consumption in hypertension, or managing weight to reduce the strain on respiratory functions in asthma.
- **Exercise**: Regular physical activity can help control blood sugar levels, reduce hypertension, and improve overall cardiovascular health. Specific exercise plans should be tailored to each patient's condition, age, and general health.
- **Smoking Cessation**: Particularly for patients with asthma or cardiovascular diseases, quitting smoking is one of the most beneficial lifestyle changes.

Educating patients about the impact of these lifestyle choices on their health conditions and providing practical advice for making sustainable changes is vital.

Preventative Measures

For infectious diseases, prevention plays a key role in management:

- **Vaccinations**: Immunizations are crucial for preventing diseases like influenza and COVID-19, reducing both the severity and spread of infections.
- **Hygiene Practices**: Regular handwashing, proper mask usage during outbreaks, and safe food practices are simple yet effective methods to prevent infection.
- **Public Health Measures**: Community-wide actions such as public education campaigns, sanitation improvements, and outbreak readiness can help manage and prevent the spread of infectious diseases.

Preventive measures not only help manage individual health but also protect public health by reducing the transmission and impact of infectious diseases.

Integration of Management Strategies

Effective disease management often requires an integrated approach that combines medical treatment, lifestyle adjustments, and preventive measures. Regular follow-up and monitoring are essential to assess the effectiveness of management strategies and make adjustments as needed. Healthcare providers should work closely with patients to develop personalized management plans that address the specific needs and challenges of each condition.

The management of common diseases is a multifaceted endeavor that involves a combination of medical interventions, lifestyle changes, and preventive measures. By understanding and implementing comprehensive management strategies, healthcare professionals can significantly improve the outcomes and quality of life for patients with chronic and infectious diseases. This section not only underscores the importance of tailored treatment plans but also highlights the role of preventive care in the broader context of healthcare. As we move forward, continuing education and adaptation to new research findings will remain key in evolving these strategies to meet the changing healthcare landscape.

Chronic Conditions: Diabetes and Hypertension

Chronic conditions such as diabetes and hypertension are major public health challenges worldwide, affecting millions of people and imposing significant health and economic burdens. These conditions require ongoing medical care and can significantly impact quality of life. Understanding the pathophysiology, signs, symptoms, and management strategies of these diseases is crucial for effective treatment and prevention. This section delves deeply into diabetes and hypertension, two prevalent chronic conditions, to provide a thorough understanding necessary for their management.

Diabetes

Diabetes is a complex group of diseases characterized by high glucose levels that, over time, can lead to serious damage to the heart, blood vessels, eyes, kidneys, and nerves. There are three main types of diabetes:

- **Type 1 Diabetes**: Often diagnosed in children and young adults, Type 1 diabetes is an autoimmune condition where the body attacks insulin-producing beta cells in the pancreas, leading to insulin deficiency. Management requires lifelong insulin therapy.
- **Type 2 Diabetes**: The most common form of diabetes, Type 2, is primarily due to the body's ineffective use of insulin, often exacerbated by excess body weight and physical inactivity. It can be managed with lifestyle changes and medications, but may also require insulin.
- **Gestational Diabetes**: This type occurs during pregnancy and usually disappears after delivery, but it increases the risk of developing Type 2 diabetes later in life.

Pathophysiology: In all types of diabetes, the underlying issue involves problems with insulin secretion, insulin action, or both, leading to hyperglycemia. **Signs and Symptoms**: Common symptoms include frequent urination, excessive thirst, extreme hunger, sudden weight loss, fatigue, blurred vision, and slow-healing wounds. **Management**: Critical elements include monitoring blood glucose levels, adopting a healthy diet, regular physical activity, medication adherence, and regular medical check-ups.

Hypertension

Hypertension, or high blood pressure, is a condition in which the blood pressure in the arteries is persistently elevated. Without proper management, hypertension can lead to atherosclerosis, heart disease, stroke, kidney damage, and other serious health issues.

Pathophysiology: Hypertension often develops with no single identifiable cause but is influenced by both genetic and lifestyle factors. It results from the increased resistance to blood flow through the arteries, which puts extra strain on the cardiovascular system. **Signs and Symptoms**: Hypertension is often called the "silent killer" because it may not exhibit noticeable symptoms until significant damage has occurred. When symptoms do appear, they may include headaches, shortness of breath, nosebleeds, or flushing. **Management**: Managing hypertension involves lifestyle modifications such as adopting a healthy diet (low in salt, saturated fats, and cholesterol), regular physical activity, weight control, and avoiding tobacco use. Many individuals also require one or more medications to control their blood pressure effectively.

Understanding diabetes and hypertension in depth helps healthcare providers manage these diseases more effectively. For both conditions, education on lifestyle changes, coupled with regular monitoring and medication management, can significantly improve patient outcomes and reduce the risk of complications. This exploration not only reinforces the importance of comprehensive care in managing chronic conditions but also highlights the need for ongoing research and education to adapt to evolving therapeutic practices. As we continue to navigate through the complexities of these conditions in subsequent sections, the integration of current knowledge with practical management strategies will remain central to improving the lives of those affected.

Respiratory and Infectious Diseases: Asthma, Influenza, and COVID-19

Respiratory and infectious diseases such as asthma, influenza, and COVID-19 present significant challenges to global public health. These conditions not only impact millions of people annually but also strain healthcare systems, especially during peaks in infectious outbreaks. Understanding the triggers, symptomatology, management, and containment strategies for these diseases is crucial for effective treatment and prevention. This section provides an in-depth look at asthma and the infectious diseases influenza and COVID-19, highlighting their clinical features, management strategies, and public health implications.

Asthma

Asthma is a chronic respiratory condition characterized by episodes of airway inflammation and bronchoconstriction that cause difficulty breathing. Key aspects include:

- **Triggers**: Asthma attacks can be triggered by a variety of factors including allergens (pollen, dust mites), irritants (smoke, pollution), respiratory infections, physical activity, and weather changes. Identifying and avoiding these triggers is a critical component of asthma management.
- **Symptomatology**: Common symptoms include wheezing, shortness of breath, chest tightness, and coughing, particularly at night or early in the morning.
- **Management Strategies**: Long-term management involves the use of controller medications such as inhaled corticosteroids and long-acting beta-agonists to reduce inflammation and prevent flare-ups. Rescue inhalers

(short-acting beta-agonists) are used to provide quick relief from acute symptoms.

- **Environmental and Lifestyle Modifications**: Improving air quality in the home and workplace and maintaining a healthy lifestyle can help reduce the frequency and severity of asthma attacks.

Influenza and COVID-19

Influenza and COVID-19 are viral respiratory infections with significant overlap in their mode of spread and public health response, yet they also exhibit distinct differences in their clinical manifestations and global impact.

- **Spread and Impact**:
- **Influenza**: Spreads mainly through droplets from coughs and sneezes. Annual outbreaks, known as seasonal flu, typically result in high morbidity but relatively low mortality compared to COVID-19.
- **COVID-19**: Caused by the SARS-CoV-2 virus, it spreads not only through respiratory droplets but also potentially via aerosols in closed environments. It has led to global pandemics with higher morbidity and mortality rates, stressing healthcare systems worldwide.
- **Containment Strategies**:
- Both diseases require robust public health strategies including social distancing, mask-wearing, and hand hygiene to control spread. Testing and contact tracing are critical for identifying and isolating cases to prevent transmission.
- **Vaccination Efforts**:
- **Influenza**: Annual vaccines are developed to match circulating strains of the flu virus. Vaccination is recommended for the entire population, especially high-risk groups.

- **COVID-19**: Vaccines have been developed at an unprecedented pace, with ongoing global distribution aimed at achieving herd immunity. Vaccine efficacy and adaptations to emerging variants continue to be monitored closely.
- **Global Surveillance Systems**:
- The importance of global health surveillance has been underscored by both diseases. Enhanced surveillance helps track disease spread, variant evolution, and the effectiveness of public health interventions.

Asthma, influenza, and COVID-19 each pose unique challenges that require tailored clinical and public health approaches. For asthma, management focuses on trigger avoidance and pharmacotherapy, whereas for influenza and COVID-19, prevention through vaccination and public health measures are paramount. This detailed examination of these respiratory and infectious diseases not only enhances understanding and preparedness but also underscores the importance of ongoing research, patient education, and global cooperation in tackling such significant health threats. As healthcare systems continue to adapt to these challenges, the lessons learned will be invaluable in shaping future responses to respiratory and infectious diseases.

Chapter 4
Medical Specialties and Personnel

Chapter 4 delves into the intricate world of medical specialties and the diverse roles of healthcare personnel. This chapter is designed to provide a detailed understanding of the various medical specialties, each dedicated to particular aspects of patient care, and to elucidate the specific terminologies and concepts unique to each specialty. Additionally, it explores the wide array of healthcare personnel, detailing their roles, responsibilities, and the specific language associated with their professions. This comprehensive overview is crucial for medical professionals, students, and anyone interested in the operational and collaborative framework of healthcare systems.

Exploring Medical Specialties

Medical specialties are focused areas of medicine that professionals dedicate their careers to, ranging from general practice to more specific areas like neurology, cardiology, or dermatology. Each specialty is defined by its unique body of knowledge, set of skills, and specific patient care objectives:

- **Defining Each Specialty**: This section will outline the major medical specialties, providing insights into the scope and focus of each field.
- **Terminology and Diagnostic Tools**: Understanding the specialized terminology used within each specialty is vital for accurate diagnosis, treatment, and communication within and across these fields.

Understanding Medical Personnel

The effective delivery of healthcare services relies on the coordinated efforts of a diverse team of medical personnel. Each member plays a pivotal role, from initial patient contact to treatment and ongoing care management:

- **Roles Across Healthcare Settings**: This section will categorize various healthcare roles, from doctors and nurses to allied health professionals like physiotherapists and pharmacists.
- **Specialized Terminology**: It will also cover the specific terms and jargon used by different healthcare personnel, essential for clear communication and effective professional practice.

Objectives of Chapter 5

- **Facilitate Interdisciplinary Understanding**: By providing a clear understanding of the roles and specialized knowledge of various medical personnel and specialties, this chapter aims to foster better communication and collaboration within the healthcare sector.
- **Educational Resource for Aspiring Professionals**: For students and new entrants into the medical field, this chapter serves as a vital educational

tool, offering a clear view of the potential career paths and their requirements.

- **Enhance Patient Care**: By demystifying the functions and terminologies of different specialties and roles, healthcare providers can ensure more informed, efficient, and compassionate patient care.

Conclusion of the Introduction

As we venture through Chapter 5, readers will gain a robust understanding of the complex landscape of medical specialties and the critical roles played by various healthcare personnel. This exploration will not only illuminate the paths of specialization within medical practice but also highlight how each specialty and role contributes to a cohesive healthcare experience, ultimately enhancing patient outcomes and operational efficiency. This foundational knowledge is indispensable for those navigating the multifaceted realms of healthcare, whether as a provider, a student, or a policy-maker.

Comprehensive Exploration of Medical Specialties
Introduction to Medical Specialties

Medical specialties are distinct branches within the field of medicine where healthcare professionals focus their practice on specific areas of patient care, diseases, and conditions. Each specialty requires a unique body of knowledge, specialized skills, and a dedicated approach to patient care. This section aims to provide a systematic exploration of various medical specialties, offering insights into their roles, the terminologies they use, and the diagnostic tools that are fundamental to each specialty. This knowledge is essential for students and professionals to understand the complexities of human anatomy, disease processes, and the collaborative nature of healthcare.

Defining Major Medical Specialties

Medical Terminology Study Guide

In the complex field of healthcare, medical specialties are categorized based on the nature of treatment, the types of diseases they address, and the specific skills required by the healthcare professionals. Each specialty focuses on a particular aspect of patient care, contributing uniquely to the comprehensive management of health. This section provides an in-depth look into surgical, medical, and other specialized fields, highlighting their roles, the diseases they commonly manage, and the skills required for each.

Surgical Specialties

Surgical specialties involve the use of operative procedures to treat diseases, injuries, and deformities. These specialties require rigorous training in surgical techniques and patient management both pre- and post-operation:

- **General Surgery**: Focuses on abdominal contents including esophagus, stomach, small bowel, colon, liver, pancreas, gallbladder, appendix, and bile ducts, as well as diseases involving the skin, breast, soft tissue, and hernias.
- **Neurosurgery**: Specializes in the surgical treatment of disorders affecting the brain, spinal cord, peripheral nerves, and extra-cranial cerebrovascular system.
- **Orthopedic Surgery**: Deals with conditions involving the musculoskeletal system. Orthopedic surgeons treat bone fractures, degenerative diseases, and sports injuries, often using both surgical and nonsurgical means.
- **Cardiovascular Surgery**: Involves the surgical treatment of disorders of the heart and blood vessels. This specialty manages complex cardiac conditions such as coronary artery disease and heart valve problems through procedures like bypass surgery and valve repair or replacement.

Medical Specialties

Medical specialties focus on the diagnosis and non-surgical treatment of diseases, utilizing medications, lifestyle adjustments, and other medical interventions:

- **Cardiology**: Deals with disorders of the heart as well as some parts of the circulatory system. The specialty is crucial for managing conditions such as hypertension, coronary artery disease, heart arrhythmias, and heart failures.
- **Neurology**: Focuses on disorders of the nervous system. Neurologists manage conditions like epilepsy, stroke, multiple sclerosis, and Parkinson's disease.
- **Gastroenterology**: Concerned with diseases affecting the gastrointestinal tract, which include the organs from mouth to anus. Gastroenterologists treat conditions such as GERD, stomach ulcers, irritable bowel syndrome, and Crohn's disease.
- **Endocrinology**: Specializes in diagnosing and treating diseases that affect the glands. Endocrinologists manage disorders like diabetes, thyroid diseases, metabolic disorders, and more.

Other Specialties

These specialties often focus on specific patient demographics or broader aspects of health and well-being:

- **Psychiatry**: Deals with the diagnosis, treatment, and prevention of mental, emotional, and behavioral disorders. Psychiatrists use therapeutic techniques, medications, and other interventions to treat conditions such as depression, schizophrenia, and anxiety disorders.
- **Dermatology**: Specializes in skin, hair, and nails. Dermatologists treat a variety of skin conditions, from acne and eczema to skin cancer.

- **Pediatrics**: Focuses on the physical, emotional, and social health of children from birth to young adulthood. Pediatricians diagnose and treat infections, injuries, genetic defects, and organic diseases and dysfunctions.

Each medical specialty is essential for the comprehensive care and management of patients with specific health needs. Understanding the scope and focus of each specialty helps healthcare providers deliver targeted and effective treatment. For students and professionals in the medical field, gaining a deep understanding of these specialties enhances their ability to make informed decisions about their career paths and improves their capability to collaborate across disciplines, ensuring holistic patient care and optimal health outcomes. This exploration into medical specialties sets the stage for further discussions on the specific roles and responsibilities of various medical personnel within these fields.

Terminology and Diagnostic Tools Specific to Each Specialty

Understanding the specific terminology and diagnostic tools used in various medical specialties is crucial for accurate diagnosis and effective treatment. This section expands on the terminology and key diagnostic tools relevant to specialties such as cardiology, neurology, dermatology, and psychiatry. Each specialty employs a unique set of terms and instruments that reflect its specific focus and patient care objectives.

Cardiology

- **Terminology**:
- **Arrhythmia**: Refers to any disturbance in the normal

sequence of the electrical impulses of the heart, which can result in irregular heartbeats.

- **Myocardial Infarction**: Commonly known as a heart attack, this occurs when blood flow to a part of the heart is blocked for a long enough time that part of the heart muscle is damaged or dies.
- **Angioplasty**: A procedure to restore blood flow through the artery by inflating a tiny balloon in a blocked artery.
- **Diagnostic Tools**:
- **Echocardiograms**: Use sound waves to create images of the heart, helpful in viewing the heart beating and pumping blood.
- **Electrocardiograms (ECGs)**: Measure the electrical activity of the heart and are used to find abnormalities.
- **Cardiac Catheterization**: Involves inserting a catheter into a chamber or vessel of the heart, which can be used for diagnostic and interventional purposes.

Neurology

- **Terminology**:
- **Epilepsy**: A neurological disorder marked by sudden recurrent episodes of sensory disturbance, loss of consciousness, or convulsions.
- **Multiple Sclerosis**: An autoimmune disease that affects the brain and spinal cord, characterized by damage to the myelin sheath.
- **Cerebrovascular Accident**: Also known as a stroke, this occurs when the blood supply to part of your brain is interrupted or reduced, preventing brain tissue from getting oxygen and nutrients.
- **Diagnostic Tools**:

- **MRI Scans**: Utilized to detect brain tumors, traumatic brain injury, developmental anomalies, multiple sclerosis, stroke, dementia, infection, and the causes of headache.
- **CT Scans**: Often used in emergency cases, capable of diagnosing stroke, bleeding in the brain, and other critical conditions.
- **Electroencephalography (EEG)**: Used to find problems related to electrical activity of the brain, tracking and recording brain wave patterns.

Dermatology

- **Terminology**:
- **Dermatitis**: Inflammation of the skin that can lead to itchiness, redness, and a rash.
- **Psoriasis**: A skin disease that causes red, itchy scaly patches, most commonly on the knees, elbows, trunk, and scalp.
- **Melanoma**: The most serious type of skin cancer.
- **Diagnostic Tools**:
- **Biopsy**: Removing small pieces of skin to diagnose a range of conditions.
- **Dermoscopy**: A diagnostic tool that allows the examination of skin lesions with a dermatoscope, which can distinguish benign from malignant lesions.
- **Skin Patch Tests**: Used to identify substances that may cause an allergic reaction in a person.

Psychiatry

- **Terminology**:
- **Schizophrenia**: A mental disorder characterized by delusions, hallucinations, and other cognitive difficulties.

- **Bipolar Disorder**: A disorder associated with episodes of mood swings ranging from depressive lows to manic highs.
- **Anxiety Disorder**: A mental health disorder characterized by feelings of worry, anxiety, or fear that are strong enough to interfere with one's daily activities.
- **Diagnostic Tools**:
- **Clinical Interviews**: The primary diagnostic tool used to gather comprehensive information, assess symptoms, and develop a rapport.
- **Psychological Testing**: Includes a variety of tests that measure and observe a person's behavior to arrive at a diagnosis and guide treatment.
- **Neuroimaging**: Sometimes used to rule out other conditions that might be causing symptoms, such as tumors or stroke.

The specific terminologies and diagnostic tools used in each medical specialty are crucial for defining the scope of practice, enhancing diagnosis accuracy, and guiding effective treatment strategies. This understanding enables medical professionals to communicate more effectively across disciplines and provides a framework for comprehensive patient care. As the field of medicine continues to evolve, so too will the technologies and terminologies in these specialties, necessitating ongoing education and adaptation by healthcare professionals.

Importance of Specialized Knowledge

In the realm of healthcare, specialized knowledge—including an understanding of unique terminologies and diagnostic tools specific to each medical specialty—is indispensable. It forms the backbone of clinical accuracy and collaborative care, ensuring that professionals can make precise diagnoses, devise effective treatment plans, and foster comprehensive patient management. This section delves deeper into the reasons why specialized knowledge is critical in medical practice, highlighting its impact on patient care, professional collaboration, and healthcare outcomes.

Enhancing Diagnostic Accuracy

- **Precision in Diagnosis**: Specialized terminologies and tools enable healthcare providers to describe and identify disease processes accurately. For example, cardiologists use specific terms like "stenosis" and tools like angiograms to pinpoint the type of heart disease, which directly influences treatment options.
- **Early Detection and Intervention**: With the correct use of specialized diagnostic tools, diseases can be detected at an earlier stage, significantly improving the prognosis. For instance, dermatologists can detect early signs of melanoma using dermoscopic analysis, dramatically increasing the chances of successful treatment.

Facilitating Effective Treatment Planning

- **Tailored Treatment Approaches**: Specialized knowledge allows healthcare providers to tailor treatments to specific diseases and patient needs. An endocrinologist, for example, can modify insulin therapy for a diabetic patient based on continuous glucose monitoring results.
- **Minimizing Complications**: Accurate and early diagnosis coupled with specialized interventions can reduce the risk of complications. For example, neurologists managing epilepsy with precise medication types and doses can prevent the frequent and severe episodes that might lead to broader health issues.

Enhancing Communication in Multidisciplinary Teams

- **Interprofessional Collaboration**: In settings where various specialists collaborate, such as hospitals or multidisciplinary clinics, understanding each other's terminologies and diagnostic approaches is vital for seamless patient care. For instance, when a cardiologist refers a patient to a nephrologist for hypertension management, both must share a common understanding of terms like 'renovascular hypertension' to ensure coherent care.
- **Standardized Patient Records**: Using specialized terminology in medical records ensures that information is accurately conveyed across different health professionals, which is crucial for ongoing patient management and when new team members are introduced to a patient's care.

Empowering Patient Engagement and Education

- **Improved Patient Communication**: Educating patients about their conditions using clear and accurate terms helps them understand their health status and the necessity of prescribed treatments. This clarity can enhance patient compliance and engagement.
- **Informed Decision Making**: Patients who understand the specifics of their diagnoses and treatment options are better equipped to make informed decisions regarding their health care. This is particularly important in specialties like oncology or surgery, where treatment decisions can significantly impact quality of life.

The importance of specialized knowledge in medical specialties cannot be overstated. It is fundamental not only for ensuring clinical excellence and safety but also for facilitating interprofessional collaboration and enhancing patient outcomes. As medicine continues to advance, the need for ongoing education in specialized knowledge becomes ever more crucial. Healthcare professionals must stay abreast of the latest developments in their fields to provide the best possible care. Ultimately, specialized knowledge is a cornerstone of effective medical practice, enabling providers to offer more personalized, accurate, and effective healthcare.

The exploration of medical specialties provided here lays a foundation for a deeper understanding of the diverse fields within medicine. By comprehensively studying the structure, function, and terminology associated with each specialty, healthcare professionals and students can enhance their ability to work collaboratively in a complex healthcare environment, ensuring better patient outcomes and advancing their careers in their chosen fields. As we continue into the next sections, this foundational knowledge will be instrumental in further discussions about medical personnel and their roles within these specialties.

Comprehensive Exploration of Understanding Medical Personnel

Introduction to Medical Personnel

The healthcare industry relies on a vast and diverse array of professionals who contribute to the delivery of medical care at every level. From the front-line providers who see patients daily to the specialists who offer advanced care, and the allied health professionals who support treatment and recovery, each role is critical. This section aims to provide a detailed understanding of the various roles within healthcare settings, their specific responsibilities, and the specialized terminology they use. This knowledge is essential for students and current healthcare professionals to appreciate the scope of medical practice and the collaborative nature of healthcare.

Roles Across Healthcare Settings

Healthcare settings feature a complex interplay of various professional roles, each contributing uniquely to patient care. From direct medical treatment to support and administrative duties, the effective functioning of healthcare systems depends on the collaborative efforts of a diverse range of professionals. This expanded section will delve deeper into the specific responsibilities, necessary skills, and crucial impact of each major group within the healthcare ecosystem.

Detailed Overview of Key Healthcare Roles

- **Doctors (Physicians):**
- **Role and Responsibilities**: Doctors are at the forefront of medical care, responsible for diagnosing illnesses, prescribing treatments, and managing patient care. They make critical decisions that can significantly affect patient outcomes.
- **Specialization**: Physicians specialize in various fields that require distinct knowledge and skills. For instance, cardiologists focus on heart-related ailments, while neurosurgeons handle complex surgeries involving the nervous system.
- **Training and Expertise**: Becoming a physician requires extensive education, including medical school, residency, and often fellowship training for highly specialized fields.
- **Nurses:**
- **Versatile Care Providers**: Nurses are integral to patient care, involved in everything from initial assessments to the implementation of ongoing care plans. They manage daily patient care, administer medications, and monitor patient status.

- **Specialized Roles**: Advanced practice nurses, like Nurse Practitioners (NPs) and Clinical Nurse Specialists (CNS), have responsibilities that overlap significantly with those of doctors, including the ability to diagnose conditions and prescribe medications.
- **Education and Certification**: Nurses must complete rigorous nursing programs and are often required to pass national licensing exams. Advanced roles require further education, such as a master's or doctoral degree.
- **Allied Health Professionals**:
- **Diverse Roles and Responsibilities**: This group encompasses a wide range of health professionals who support, facilitate, and complement the work of doctors and nurses.
- **Physiotherapists**: Help patients recover physical function and manage pain through therapeutic exercises, manipulations, and other treatments.
- **Pharmacists**: Manage and dispense medications, providing advice on drug dosages, side effects, and interactions.
- **Radiologists and Laboratory Technicians**: Play critical roles in diagnosis by performing and interpreting various diagnostic tests such as X-rays, MRIs, and blood tests.
- **Specialized Training**: Each role requires specialized training and certification. For example, physiotherapists need a degree in physical therapy and must pass a licensure exam.
- **Support Staff**:
- **Foundational Role in Healthcare**: Support staff, including medical assistants, healthcare administrators, and clerical workers, ensure the smooth operation of healthcare facilities.

- **Tasks and Responsibilities**: Their duties range from scheduling appointments and managing patient records to supporting medical billing and coding.
- **Training and Skills**: Positions vary from requiring specific certifications (e.g., for medical assistants) to on-the-job training for administrative roles.

The Impact of Professional Collaboration in Healthcare

- **Enhanced Patient Care**: The collaborative efforts of these diverse roles ensure comprehensive care that addresses all aspects of a patient's health, from prevention and diagnosis to treatment and rehabilitation.
- **Efficiency and Effectiveness**: Effective collaboration among healthcare professionals can lead to more efficient use of resources, shorter hospital stays, and better health outcomes.
- **Continuity of Care**: Seamless communication and collaboration among different healthcare providers support continuity of care, which is crucial for treating chronic conditions and ensuring effective long-term care.

Understanding the roles of various healthcare professionals within medical settings provides valuable insights into how health services are delivered and managed. It highlights the importance of each role in ensuring effective and efficient patient care. As the healthcare field continues to evolve, the integration of new technologies and methodologies will likely expand and redefine these roles further, emphasizing the need for ongoing education and adaptive collaboration in this dynamic field.

· · ·

Specialized Terminology Used by Medical Personnel

Effective communication in healthcare is not just about exchanging information; it's about doing so with precision and clarity. Specialized medical terminology is essential for this purpose, as it provides a common language that helps ensure clear understanding among medical professionals and supports accurate documentation. This section will explore in detail the specialized terms used by various healthcare personnel, from doctors and nurses to allied health professionals and radiologists.

Specialized Terminology Used by Doctors and Nurses

- **Doctors**: Physicians across various specialties use specific terminologies that relate to their field of expertise. For instance:
- **Cardiologists** might use terms like "myocardial infarction" (heart attack) and "arrhythmia" (irregular heartbeat).
- **Neurologists** often refer to "neuroplasticity" (the ability of neural networks in the brain to change through growth and reorganization) and "cerebrovascular accident" (stroke).
- **Nurses**: While they share many terms with doctors, nurses also use terminologies that reflect their caregiving perspective, such as:
- **PRN** (from the Latin "pro re nata," meaning "as needed"), which is used in prescribing medicine.
- **Triage**, which refers to the process of determining the priority of patients' treatments based on the severity of their condition.

Terminology Specific to Allied Health Professionals

- **Physiotherapists**: These professionals use terms that relate to physical therapy and rehabilitation, such as:
- **Manual Therapy**: Techniques involving hands-on manipulation of the musculoskeletal system.
- **Therapeutic Exercise**: Exercises tailored to treat specific physical issues to improve movement and strength.
- **Pharmacists**: In their role, pharmacists discuss terms that concern the pharmacodynamics and pharmacokinetics of medications, including:
- **Bioavailability**: The degree and rate at which a drug is absorbed into the bloodstream, available for use or storage in the body.
- **Half-life**: The time required for the concentration of a drug in the body to be reduced by half, critical for understanding dosing schedules.

Terminology Used by Radiologists

- **Radiologists** and imaging technicians utilize a set of terms specific to imaging diagnostics, such as:
- **Radiopaque**: Materials that do not permit X-rays or similar radiation to pass through, appearing white or light on radiographs.
- **Angiography**: A diagnostic test that uses X-rays to take pictures of the blood vessels after injecting a contrast material that is radiopaque to highlight conditions such as blockages or malformed arteries and veins.

The Importance of Understanding Specialized Terminology

- **Improved Patient Care**: Accurate use of medical

terminology enhances the precision in diagnosis and treatment plans, leading to better patient outcomes.

- **Enhanced Communication**: Clear and effective use of specialized terms ensures that all healthcare providers, regardless of their specific roles, can understand and collaborate effectively, reducing errors and improving efficiency.
- **Patient Education and Engagement**: When healthcare providers can explain conditions and treatments correctly using understandable terms, it increases patient engagement and adherence to treatment protocols.

The use of specialized medical terminology is a foundational aspect of healthcare that ensures effective communication and enhances clinical accuracy. By understanding and correctly applying these terms, healthcare professionals of all kinds improve their ability to deliver quality care. As medical science advances, the vocabulary will continue to evolve, underscoring the need for ongoing education and training in the language of medicine. This section has illuminated the critical role that specialized terminology plays across various disciplines within healthcare, highlighting its importance in the broader medical ecosystem.

Importance of Specialized Knowledge in Healthcare Roles

In the multifaceted world of healthcare, specialized knowledge forms the bedrock of professional efficacy and collaborative practice. This knowledge is not only pivotal in enhancing patient care but also crucial in facilitating professional interactions and advancing careers within the healthcare industry. This section delves into the significance of specialized knowledge, particularly the understanding and application of specific terminologies pertinent to various healthcare roles.

Enhanced Patient Care

- **Precision in Clinical Practice**: Specialized knowledge, especially in understanding medical terminology, enables healthcare providers to accurately diagnose and treat conditions. This precision is fundamental in developing effective treatment plans tailored to individual patient needs, thereby directly enhancing the quality of patient care.
- **Reduction in Errors**: A deep understanding of specialized medical terms minimizes the likelihood of misinterpretations that can lead to clinical errors. Clear and precise communication, powered by a thorough grasp of terminology, is essential in complex clinical settings where the margin for error is small.
- **Patient Trust and Compliance**: When healthcare providers use specialized terms correctly and explain them effectively to patients, it builds trust. Patients who understand their health situations are more likely to comply with treatment plans, leading to better health outcomes.

Professional Collaboration

- **Seamless Teamwork**: In an environment as collaborative as healthcare, where multidisciplinary teams are the norm, specialized knowledge ensures that all team members are on the same page. For example, when a surgeon and an anesthesiologist discuss a patient's preoperative status, both must understand the specific risks and terminology associated with the surgical procedure and anesthesia.

- **Efficient Resource Utilization**: Effective communication facilitated by specialized knowledge helps in the efficient use of resources. Clear discussions about patient care plans reduce redundancy and enhance the efficacy of interventions.
- **Interdepartmental Coordination**: In hospitals and larger healthcare settings, coordination across various departments—such as radiology, pharmacy, and nursing—relies heavily on everyone's understanding of specific medical terminologies and procedures.

Educational and Career Advancement

- **Professional Growth**: For healthcare professionals, mastering specialized terminology is not just about immediate clinical responsibilities; it's also crucial for long-term career development. Knowledge and proficiency in specific medical languages often set the foundation for advancing into specialist roles or leadership positions.
- **Lifelong Learning**: The field of medicine is ever-evolving, with new terms, treatments, and technologies continually emerging. Ongoing education and familiarity with current and specialized knowledge are essential for staying relevant in the profession.
- **Credentialing and Certification**: Many healthcare roles require certifications that necessitate a deep understanding of specialized knowledge. Success in these certifications opens doors to new opportunities and is often a prerequisite for practicing in specialized fields.

The importance of specialized knowledge in healthcare cannot be overstated. It is crucial for enhancing patient care, facilitating professional collaboration, and driving educational and career advancement. As healthcare continues to evolve with advancements in medicine and technology, the demand for professionals who are not only skilled but also deeply knowledgeable in their specific areas will continue to grow. This emphasis on specialized knowledge underscores the commitment to excellence and safety in healthcare, ensuring that all professionals are equipped to meet the challenges and opportunities of their roles effectively.

The array of roles within the healthcare sector is as diverse as the field itself, each contributing to the overall goal of patient health and wellbeing. Understanding these roles and the specialized terminology associated with them is crucial for anyone involved in healthcare, whether they are entering the field, currently practicing, or involved in the management and coordination of healthcare services. As the field continues to evolve with advancements in medicine and technology, the need for skilled professionals across all these roles will continue to grow, highlighting the importance of comprehensive education and ongoing professional development in the healthcare industry.

Chapter 5 has provided an extensive exploration of the diverse roles and specialized knowledge inherent in the medical field. By delving deeply into the various medical specialties and the personnel who drive these disciplines, this chapter has aimed to illuminate the complexities and intricacies of healthcare delivery. Each section has been crafted to enhance understanding of how different professionals contribute uniquely to patient care, emphasizing the importance of interdisciplinary collaboration, precise communication, and targeted education.

The objectives set out at the beginning of the chapter—to facilitate interdisciplinary understanding, provide a robust educational resource, and enhance patient care—have been addressed through detailed descriptions, practical examples, and the elucidation of specialized terminology. These elements work collectively to foster a healthcare environment where professionals are well-prepared to meet the challenges of their roles, equipped with knowledge that enhances their capacity for decision-making and patient interaction.

Building upon the foundational knowledge of medical specialties and personnel, we now transition to Chapter 6: Hospital Departments and Services. This next chapter shifts focus from the broad roles and specialties within the healthcare workforce to the specific operational segments and services that form the backbone of hospital infrastructure.

Chapter 5
Hospital Departments and Services

Chapter 5 will provide a detailed overview of how hospitals are structured and operate, focusing on the various departments and services that are critical to both daily functions and exceptional circumstances. Each hospital department—from Emergency Services and Radiology to Surgery and Pediatrics—plays a pivotal role in the healthcare delivery system, offering specialized care that is critical to patient outcomes.

- **Overview of Hospital Departments**: This section will explore major hospital departments, detailing the specific functions, services, and coordination mechanisms that define their operations. Understanding the role of each department helps clarify how hospitals provide comprehensive care across different medical specialties.
- **Integration of Services**: Hospitals are more than a collection of independent departments; they are integrated systems where services and information flow continuously to ensure efficient, effective patient care.

This chapter will examine how these departments interact, share information, and collaborate to handle patient needs seamlessly.

- **Operational Challenges and Solutions**: Managing a hospital's departments involves addressing numerous operational challenges, from resource allocation to process optimization. This section will discuss innovative solutions and management practices that contribute to smooth hospital operations and high-quality patient care.

In conclusion, as we move forward into Chapter 6, we aim to unpack the structural and functional aspects of hospital departments and services, providing insights that are essential for anyone engaged in or aspiring to work within a hospital setting. This chapter will not only augment the understanding of hospital operations but also showcase how these entities are essential components of the healthcare system, ensuring that all patients receive the care they need in a timely and efficient manner.

Comprehensive Exploration of Hospital Departments

Hospital departments are fundamental units within a hospital that specialize in specific areas of patient care, diagnostics, and treatment. Each department is equipped with specialized personnel and equipment tailored to their specific medical or administrative focus. This section aims to provide an in-depth overview of the major hospital departments, examining their roles, functions, and how they integrate within the overall hospital system to ensure comprehensive patient care.

Detailed Overview of Key Hospital Departments

The Emergency Department (ED) serves as the frontline of hospital care, addressing immediate and urgent medical needs. It is a critical component of any hospital, designed to respond swiftly to a wide range of medical emergencies. This section aims to provide a detailed overview of the ED's function, the services it offers, and its role in the broader hospital ecosystem through coordination with other departments.

Function of the Emergency Department

- **Immediate Care Provision**: The primary function of the ED is to provide rapid assessment and treatment to patients presenting with acute illnesses or injuries. This unit is pivotal in stabilizing patients in life-threatening conditions, ensuring they receive care at the most critical times.
- **24/7 Operation**: Unlike other hospital departments that may have more predictable schedules, the ED operates around the clock, every day of the year. This constant readiness is essential to address the unpredictable nature of emergencies.
- **Handling a Spectrum of Emergencies**: EDs are equipped to handle everything from minor injuries to major, life-threatening conditions such as heart attacks, strokes, severe trauma, and other critical conditions.

Services Provided by the Emergency Department

- **Triage**: This is the initial assessment process in the ED, where patients are quickly evaluated based on the severity of their conditions. Triage ensures that those who need urgent care receive immediate attention, prioritizing patients based on the urgency of their needs.
- **Urgent Treatment**: After triage, patients receive the necessary urgent care. This can include administration of pain relief, wound care, setting fractures, or more complex procedures required to stabilize the patient.

- **Life-Saving Interventions**: The ED is equipped with the technology and expertise to perform life-saving procedures such as advanced cardiac life support, emergency intubation, and administration of emergency medications.

Coordination with Other Hospital Departments

- **Seamless Transfers**: Once patients are stabilized, they may need to be transferred to other departments for further treatment or observation. For example, a patient who has had a heart attack might be moved to the cardiology unit for ongoing care.
- **Information Sharing**: Effective communication systems are essential in the ED to ensure that patient information is quickly and accurately shared with other departments. This coordination supports the continuity of care as patients move through different parts of the hospital.
- **Interdepartmental Support**: The ED often relies on support from other departments such as radiology for diagnostic imaging, laboratory services for urgent testing, and surgery for immediate surgical interventions.

Challenges and Innovations in Emergency Department Operations

- **Overcrowding**: One of the significant challenges in many EDs is overcrowding, which can lead to delayed care and increased stress on staff and resources.
- **Innovative Solutions**: To combat challenges like overcrowding, many hospitals have introduced systems such as fast-track services for less severe cases,

telemedicine consultations to reduce physical visits, and improved patient flow processes to enhance efficiency.

The Emergency Department is a vital component of hospital operations, designed to deliver rapid and effective medical interventions during critical times. Understanding the detailed functioning, services, and coordination mechanisms of the ED is essential for all healthcare professionals working in or with these units. By optimizing the efficiency and effectiveness of emergency services, hospitals can ensure better patient outcomes and improve the overall quality of care provided. As healthcare continues to evolve, so too will the strategies for managing and enhancing the services offered by Emergency Departments.

- **Surgery Department**

The Surgery Department is a pivotal component of hospital care, dedicated to performing surgical interventions to treat a range of diseases, injuries, and deformities. This department plays a crucial role in the overall treatment plan for many patients, offering solutions that other medical treatments cannot provide. This section aims to delve into the function of the Surgery Department, the variety of services it offers, and its critical interactions with other hospital departments to ensure holistic patient care.

Function of the Surgery Department

- **Purpose and Role**: The primary function of the Surgery Department is to conduct surgical procedures that are essential for diagnosing, treating, or managing various health issues. This includes surgeries that can be planned well in advance (elective surgeries) and those that must be performed immediately (emergency surgeries).

- **Surgical Expertise**: Surgeons in this department are highly trained to perform operations that require precision and specialized technical skills to ensure successful outcomes for patients.
- **Facilities and Equipment**: The department is equipped with state-of-the-art surgical facilities that include operating rooms, pre-operative and post-operative care areas, and specialized surgical equipment.

Services Provided by the Surgery Department

- **Types of Surgeries**:
- **General Surgery**: Encompasses a wide range of surgical procedures that involve the abdominal organs, breast, thyroid, and other soft tissues.
- **Orthopedic Surgery**: Focuses on surgeries related to bones, joints, and muscles, often addressing injuries and chronic conditions like arthritis or back pain.
- **Cardiovascular Surgery**: Involves complex surgeries on the heart and blood vessels to treat conditions such as heart disease and vascular disorders.
- **Comprehensive Care**:
- **Pre-Operative Assessment**: Prior to any surgical procedure, a thorough evaluation of the patient's health is performed to ensure they are fit for surgery and to plan the best surgical approach.
- **Surgical Intervention**: The core service of the department where the actual surgeries are performed using various techniques, from minimally invasive, such as laparoscopic surgery, to major open surgeries.
- **Post-Operative Care**: After surgery, patients are moved to recovery areas where they receive continuous

monitoring and care to manage pain, prevent infections, and ensure proper healing.

Coordination with Other Hospital Departments

- **Anesthesia**: Works in close collaboration with anesthesiologists who provide pain management during and after surgeries. This collaboration is crucial for the safety and comfort of the patient throughout the surgical process.
- **Post-Operative Recovery Units**: These specialized units care for patients immediately following surgery. Coordination ensures that patients are safely transitioned from the operating room to recovery rooms where they receive tailored care.
- **Intensive Care Units (ICUs)**: For more complex surgeries that involve significant risks or recovery challenges, patients may need to be admitted to the ICU. The Surgery Department coordinates closely with ICU staff to provide continuous, intensive care for post-surgical patients.
- **Radiology and Laboratory Services**: Often, surgical procedures require pre-operative and post-operative diagnostic tests, including imaging and laboratory tests, to guide the surgical process and assess post-surgical recovery.

Challenges and Innovations

- **Managing Surgical Risks**: Surgery departments continually seek to minimize the risks associated with surgical procedures, such as infections, complications from anesthesia, and post-operative complications.

- **Technological Advancements**: Incorporating new technologies such as robotic surgery and image-guided surgery enhances precision and reduces recovery times, revolutionizing how surgeries are performed.

The Surgery Department is essential for providing critical interventions that are vital for patient care within the hospital setting. Understanding the depth and breadth of surgical services, along with the department's coordination with other hospital units, highlights its integral role in comprehensive healthcare. As medical technology advances, the scope and effectiveness of surgical interventions continue to evolve, underscoring the department's continuous commitment to improving patient outcomes and enhancing the quality of care.

- **Radiology Department**

The Radiology Department is a cornerstone of modern healthcare, utilizing advanced imaging technologies to diagnose and treat a wide range of diseases. This department plays a critical role not just in visualizing the structure and function of the body's interior but also in guiding certain therapeutic procedures. This section will provide an in-depth look at the function of the Radiology Department, detail the imaging services it provides, and explore its integral role in coordinating care with other hospital departments.

Function of the Radiology Department

- **Diagnostic and Therapeutic Role**: Radiology primarily serves a diagnostic function by capturing images of the body that reveal details unseen to the naked eye. However, its role extends to therapeutic interventions, particularly through interventional radiology, which combines imaging and minimally invasive procedures to treat conditions.

- **Technological Sophistication**: The department is equipped with state-of-the-art imaging technologies that require specialized knowledge and skills to operate, ensuring high-quality diagnostic images are produced.

Services Provided by the Radiology Department

- **Diverse Imaging Modalities**:
- **X-rays**: Often the first line of imaging, used to visualize bone fractures, chest infections, and certain tumors.
- **MRI Scans (Magnetic Resonance Imaging)**: Provides detailed images of soft tissues, such as organs, muscles, brain tissue, and nerves, using powerful magnets and radio waves.
- **CT Scans (Computed Tomography)**: Offers clear, cross-sectional images of the body, including bones, blood vessels, and soft tissues, using X-rays from multiple angles.
- **Ultrasound**: Uses high-frequency sound waves to create images of the inside of the body, commonly used in obstetrics, cardiology, and to examine other soft tissues.
- **Interventional Radiology**:
- **Minimally Invasive Treatments**: Procedures such as angioplasty (widening narrowed or obstructed blood vessels), stent placement, and targeted drug delivery systems that are guided by imaging technologies.
- **Diagnostic Procedures**: Includes biopsies and fluid drainages that are performed using guidance from real-time images to ensure precision.

Coordination with Other Hospital Departments

- **Diagnostic Support**: Radiology supports nearly all departments by providing essential diagnostic images that guide further medical decisions. For instance, before a surgical procedure, a surgeon may request specific scans to determine the exact location and extent of a pathology.
- **Real-Time Imaging for Procedures**: In departments like surgery or oncology, radiologists often provide real-time imaging guidance during procedures to improve the accuracy of interventions.
- **Collaborative Care**: The department works closely with emergency services to quickly diagnose conditions that are critical and time-sensitive, such as strokes or internal injuries.

Challenges and Innovations

- **Managing Exposure Risks**: One of the ongoing challenges in radiology is managing the risk associated with exposure to radiation. This requires constant monitoring and updating of safety protocols to protect both patients and staff.
- **Advancements in Imaging Technology**: The field of radiology is continually advancing with new technologies like digital imaging, 3D imaging, and AI-enhanced diagnostics, which improve the clarity, speed, and utility of imaging studies.

The Radiology Department is an indispensable part of the hospital, offering crucial diagnostic and therapeutic services that underpin the entirety of patient care. By providing detailed visualizations of the internal workings of the body, radiology not only aids in diagnosing a vast array of conditions but also enhances the precision of treatments across various medical specialties. As technology progresses, the capabilities of radiology continue to expand, increasing the department's impact on patient outcomes and solidifying its role as a central pillar of modern medical practice.

- ## Intensive Care Unit (ICU)

The Intensive Care Unit (ICU) is a critical component of hospital care, designed to manage patients with severe and life-threatening conditions requiring continuous and comprehensive monitoring and treatment. This unit is equipped with advanced medical technology and staffed by highly trained healthcare professionals who specialize in critical care. This section will delve into the ICU's essential functions, the specialized services it provides, and its vital role in coordinating with other hospital departments to deliver life-saving care.

Function of the Intensive Care Unit

- **Critical Patient Care**: The primary function of the ICU is to provide intensive treatment to patients whose conditions are so severe that they require constant monitoring and life-support interventions. These patients may have suffered major injuries, severe infections, or are recovering from major surgeries.
- **Support for Vital Functions**: The ICU is equipped to support and, if necessary, take over the body's vital functions. This includes advanced respiratory support for patients who are unable to breathe on their own, sophisticated monitoring systems for vital signs, and specialized equipment to support other critical bodily functions.

Services Provided by the Intensive Care Unit

- **24/7 Monitoring**: Continuous monitoring is crucial for patients in the ICU. Staff use a variety of equipment to monitor heart rate, blood pressure, respiratory rate, and other vital parameters to quickly detect changes in the patient's condition.
- **Mechanical Ventilation**: This is a common and critical service in the ICU, provided to patients who are unable to breathe adequately on their own. Ventilators help maintain oxygenation and carbon dioxide removal, which are vital for life.
- **Advanced Medical Interventions**: Beyond basic life support, the ICU administers advanced drug therapies, dialysis for kidney failure, and intravenous nutrition among other specialized treatments that are often too complex to be handled in other parts of the hospital.

Coordination with Other Hospital Departments

- **Seamless Transfers**: Critically ill patients often need urgent care from various specialists. The ICU coordinates closely with departments such as the emergency room, surgery, and radiology to ensure that all aspects of a patient's care are addressed swiftly and efficiently.
- **Post-ICU Care**: Once patients stabilize, they may no longer need intensive care but still require hospitalization. The ICU works closely with departments like general medicine or step-down units to ensure a smooth transition and ongoing care.
- **Multidisciplinary Approach**: The nature of critical care often requires a multidisciplinary approach. Specialists such as pulmonologists, cardiologists, nephrologists, and others regularly collaborate with ICU

staff to provide comprehensive care tailored to each patient's complex needs.

Challenges and Innovations in ICU Management

- **Resource Intensity**: The ICU is one of the most resource-intensive parts of the hospital, requiring not just advanced equipment but also a high ratio of staff to patients. Managing these resources efficiently while maintaining high care standards is a constant challenge.
- **Technological Advancements**: Innovation in medical technology continually transforms ICU care. Developments in monitoring technology, non-invasive treatment options, and data analytics help improve patient outcomes and operational efficiency.
- **Staff Training and Wellbeing**: Given the high-stress environment of the ICU, ensuring that staff are well-trained and supported is crucial. Ongoing education, mental health support, and strategies to prevent burnout are integral to maintaining a resilient ICU team.

The Intensive Care Unit is an essential pillar of hospital infrastructure, providing lifesaving care to the most vulnerable patients. Understanding the intricate operations of the ICU, the specialized care it provides, and its integration with the rest of the hospital highlights its critical role in healthcare delivery. As medical science advances, the capabilities of the ICU continue to evolve, bringing new challenges and opportunities to enhance patient care and outcomes in this high-stakes environment.

- ## Obstetrics and Gynecology (OB/GYN)

The Obstetrics and Gynecology (OB/GYN) Department is a crucial component of hospital care, focusing specifically on women's reproductive health, pregnancy, and childbirth. This department not only manages the health concerns related to the female reproductive system but also ensures the health and safety of both mothers and their babies during and after pregnancy. This section aims to delve into the functional roles, specialized services, and collaborative efforts of the OB/GYN department.

Function of the Obstetrics and Gynecology Department

- **Specialized Medical Care**: The OB/GYN department provides specialized medical care that covers a wide range of women's health issues—from adolescent gynecology to menopause, and especially, pregnancy and childbirth.
- **Holistic Approach to Women's Health**: Beyond addressing specific medical concerns, the department also focuses on preventive health, education, and counseling, which are crucial for long-term health and well-being.

Services Provided by the Obstetrics and Gynecology Department

- **Prenatal Care**: Comprehensive care throughout pregnancy is vital for the health of both the mother and the fetus. Prenatal services include regular check-ups, ultrasound scans, genetic testing, and management of pregnancy-related conditions.
- **Labor and Delivery Services**: This includes managing and supporting all phases of childbirth—from

labor through delivery and immediate postnatal care. The department is equipped with facilities for various birthing methods and emergency interventions if needed.

- **Gynecological Services**: Apart from pregnancy-related care, the department also handles other aspects of women's reproductive health such as menstrual disorders, hormonal imbalances, pelvic pain, and other gynecological disorders.

Coordination with Other Hospital Departments

- **Collaboration with Neonatology**: The OB/GYN department works closely with Neonatology to manage the care of newborns, especially in cases of premature birth or health complications. This ensures that newborns receive specialized care that is immediately available if required.
- **Integration with Pediatrics**: This collaboration ensures a seamless transition for newborn care from the neonatal team to pediatric care, facilitating ongoing health checks and vaccinations.
- **Family Medicine Interaction**: Family medicine practitioners often collaborate with OB/GYNs for comprehensive postnatal care, focusing on the health of both the mother and the baby, ensuring they receive holistic family-centered care.

Challenges and Innovations in Obstetrics and Gynecology

- **Managing High-Risk Pregnancies**: One of the significant challenges is the management of high-risk pregnancies that may involve pre-existing health conditions, multiple gestations, or pregnancy-induced complications. Advanced monitoring and treatment strategies are crucial in these cases.

- **Advancements in Reproductive Technologies**: Innovations in medical technology, such as improved fetal monitoring systems, minimally invasive surgical techniques, and enhanced imaging technologies, continue to revolutionize the care provided in OB/GYN departments.

- **Education and Outreach**: Increasing patient education and outreach is vital for promoting reproductive health and preventive care, reducing the prevalence of complications through informed health choices.

The Obstetrics and Gynecology Department plays a vital role in ensuring the health and safety of women and newborns. Through its comprehensive care services, specialized medical attention, and collaborative efforts with related departments, the OB/GYN department embodies a holistic approach to reproductive health and childbirth. As new technologies and medical practices evolve, the department continually enhances its capacity to provide exceptional care, responding effectively to the needs of women and their families throughout the stages of pregnancy and beyond. This ensures that the OB/GYN department remains at the forefront of delivering specialized and compassionate healthcare.

- **Pediatrics Department**

The Pediatrics Department is dedicated to the medical care of infants, children, and adolescents, providing a range of services designed to manage health from the early stages of infancy through to young adulthood. This department plays a pivotal role in the prevention, diagnosis, and treatment of both acute and chronic conditions affecting children. This section aims to provide an in-depth look at the function of the Pediatrics Department, the services it offers, and its crucial role in coordinating care with other hospital departments.

Function of the Pediatrics Department

- **Child-Centered Medical Care**: Pediatrics is exclusively focused on the health and well-being of children from birth through adolescence. Pediatricians are trained to understand the unique medical needs of children, who are not merely "small adults" but have distinct physiological and psychological needs.
- **Preventative Care and Health Maintenance**: Pediatricians play a critical role in preventative care, including routine checkups, vaccinations, and health screenings, which are crucial for monitoring growth and development and preventing illness.

Services Provided by the Pediatrics Department

- **General Pediatric Care**: This includes ongoing health evaluations, treatment of common childhood illnesses, and management of minor injuries. Pediatricians also provide parental guidance regarding growth, nutrition, and developmental milestones.
- **Pediatric Subspecialties**: For more complex health issues, pediatric subspecialties offer focused expertise in areas such as:
- **Pediatric Oncology**: Treatment and management of cancers affecting children.
- **Pediatric Cardiology**: Specializing in diagnosing and treating heart conditions in children.
- **Pediatric Neurology**: Managing neurological

disorders in children, such as epilepsy, cerebral palsy, and muscular dystrophy.

- **Emergency Care**: Pediatric departments are equipped to handle emergencies that are specific to children, providing immediate care for acute medical issues.

Coordination with Other Hospital Departments

- **Collaborative Pediatric Care**: Children with complex health issues often require care that spans multiple specialties. Pediatricians coordinate closely with other departments to ensure comprehensive treatment. For example, a child with a congenital heart defect might receive care that involves both pediatric cardiology and pediatric surgery.
- **Integration with Family Medicine**: Pediatricians work alongside family medicine practitioners to ensure a continuum of care as children grow, particularly in managing chronic conditions or transitioning care plans to adult care providers.
- **Linkages with Obstetrics and Neonatology**: The Pediatrics Department works in conjunction with obstetrics and neonatology, particularly in managing preterm births or congenital anomalies identified before or at birth.

Challenges and Innovations in Pediatric Care

- **Meeting Diverse Needs**: The challenge in pediatrics is addressing a wide range of health conditions across different ages and developmental stages. Each stage from infancy to adolescence requires different approaches to communication, diagnosis, and treatment.

- **Technological Advancements**: Innovations such as digital health records tailored for pediatric use, advanced diagnostic tools, and child-friendly medical devices enhance the delivery of pediatric care.
- **Child and Family Education**: Pediatricians often take on the role of educators not just for the child, but also for the family, instructing them on health, wellness, and disease prevention strategies tailored to the child's needs.

The Pediatrics Department is integral to fostering a healthy foundation for the future of children and adolescents. By providing targeted medical care, specialized services, and comprehensive coordination with other medical departments, pediatricians play a crucial role in the health care system. As new medical advancements emerge and as the understanding of pediatric care evolves, the role of the Pediatrics Department continues to expand, ensuring that children receive the specialized care they require to thrive into healthy adulthood.

- .

- **Oncology Department**

The Oncology Department is a crucial segment of hospital care, focused exclusively on the diagnosis, treatment, and management of cancer. This department utilizes a multifaceted approach to combat various types of cancer, integrating advanced therapies and technologies to offer the best possible patient outcomes. This section will detail the specific functions of the Oncology Department, describe the comprehensive services it offers, and highlight its essential role in coordinating with other departments to provide holistic cancer care.

Function of the Oncology Department

- **Cancer Care Specialist**: The primary function of the Oncology Department is to manage all aspects of cancer treatment from the initial diagnosis through the entirety of the treatment process, including follow-up care.
- **Research and Development**: Beyond patient care, many oncology departments are also involved in cancer research, striving to develop newer and more effective treatments. This includes clinical trials that can offer patients access to cutting-edge therapies.

Services Provided by the Oncology Department

- **Chemotherapy**: Utilizes powerful drugs to target and kill cancer cells. Chemotherapy can be used as a standalone treatment or in conjunction with other therapies to improve outcomes.
- **Radiation Therapy**: Involves the use of high-energy radiation to shrink tumors and kill cancer cells. It is meticulously planned to minimize damage to surrounding healthy tissues.
- **Surgical Oncology**: Focuses on the surgical removal of tumors and cancerous tissues. This service is crucial for solid tumors that are localized and can be physically excised.
- **Immunotherapy**: Employs treatments that boost the body's natural defenses to fight the cancer.
- **Hormone Therapy**: Used particularly for cancers that are sensitive to hormones, such as breast and prostate cancer, this therapy blocks the body's ability to produce or use certain hormones.

Coordination with Other Hospital Departments

- **Radiology**: Critical for the accurate diagnosis and staging of cancers. Oncologists rely on imaging studies like CT scans, MRIs, and PET scans provided by the Radiology Department to guide the treatment planning process.
- **Surgical Departments**: For cancers requiring surgical intervention, oncology coordinates closely with various surgical specialties to plan and execute tumor-removal surgeries.
- **Palliative Care Teams**: Essential for providing support and improving the quality of life for patients undergoing cancer treatment, especially those with advanced cancer. The oncology department works alongside palliative care professionals to manage pain and other symptoms effectively.
- **Pathology**: Works closely with pathology to accurately diagnose the type of cancer and understand its genetic makeup, which can significantly influence treatment options.

Challenges and Innovations in Oncological Care

- **Personalized Medicine**: One of the significant challenges in oncology is developing personalized treatment strategies that are tailored to the individual genetic makeup of each patient's cancer. This approach aims to increase the effectiveness of treatment while reducing side effects.
- **Multidisciplinary Care Models**: Implementing a multidisciplinary approach is crucial for effective cancer care. This involves forming teams of specialists who review and discuss the medical condition and treatment options for a patient.

- **Technological Advancements**: The introduction of advanced technologies in genetic testing, robotic surgery, and targeted radiation therapy continues to revolutionize the field of oncology, offering new hopes for treatments that are less invasive and more effective.

The Oncology Department plays a vital role in a hospital's ability to combat cancer effectively. By providing a comprehensive range of specialized services and coordinating closely with other medical and surgical departments, oncology ensures that patients receive integrated, state-of-the-art care tailored to their specific needs. As research progresses and new treatments are developed, the role of the Oncology Department will continue to evolve, underscoring its importance in improving cancer outcomes and enhancing patient care across the healthcare spectrum.

Effective departmental coordination is essential for the smooth operation of a hospital and for providing patient-centered care. The interdepartmental workflow must be seamless to ensure that patients receive timely and appropriate interventions. This integration also extends to administrative departments like medical records and billing, which support the clinical sides by handling essential logistics and documentation.

The varied hospital departments form a network of specialized care that addresses every aspect of patient health, from emergency responses to specialized treatments for chronic conditions. Understanding the structure, function, and interrelation of these departments within the hospital system is crucial for healthcare professionals who aim to navigate this complex environment effectively. This detailed exploration not only serves as a guide for aspiring and current medical professionals but also enhances the overall efficiency and quality of healthcare delivery by fostering a deeper understanding of each department's role in the patient care continuum.

Comprehensive Exploration of Integration of Services in Hospitals

Hospitals are complex entities where seamless integration of various departments ensures the delivery of efficient and effective patient care. The continuous flow of services and information between departments is critical for maintaining high standards of care and for responding swiftly to patient needs. This section aims to delve into the mechanisms of how hospital departments interact, share information, and collaborate, highlighting the importance of integrated healthcare systems in achieving optimal outcomes.

Mechanisms of Service Integration

Effective integration of services is critical for ensuring that hospitals operate efficiently and deliver high-quality patient care. This section delves into the key mechanisms hospitals use to integrate services across various departments, focusing on enhancing communication, coordination, and care delivery. These mechanisms are vital for ensuring that all aspects of a patient's treatment are managed seamlessly and cohesively.

Interdepartmental Communication Systems

- **Role of Technology in Communication:** Advanced information technology systems, such as Electronic Health Records (EHRs), play a pivotal role in facilitating communication across hospital departments. EHRs allow for the real-time sharing of patient data, which is crucial for timely and informed decision-making.

- **Benefits of Real-Time Data Sharing**: With EHRs, critical patient information such as lab results, imaging studies, nursing notes, and detailed treatment plans are readily accessible to all relevant healthcare providers. This immediate access helps prevent delays in treatment, reduces the risk of errors, and enhances the overall quality of care.

Patient Care Teams

- **Multidisciplinary Approach**: Patient care teams are typically composed of various healthcare specialists including surgeons, anesthesiologists, nurses, pharmacists, and other allied health professionals. These teams embody a multidisciplinary approach to patient care, ensuring comprehensive treatment planning.
- **Regular Coordination Meetings**: These teams often meet regularly to discuss ongoing cases, share insights, and plan future interventions. These discussions ensure that each team member is aware of the patient's current status and any anticipated needs, fostering a unified approach to patient care.

Clinical Pathways and Protocols

- **Standardizing Care**: Clinical pathways and protocols are essential tools for standardizing care across hospital settings. These structured plans are developed based on best practices and evidence-based medicine to guide the clinical care of patients with specific conditions.
- **Implementation and Benefits**: By outlining critical steps in the care process, these pathways help streamline interventions, reduce variability in treatment, and improve outcomes by ensuring consistency in care across providers and shifts.

Case Management

- **Role of Case Managers**: Case managers play a crucial role in overseeing the continuum of care for patients as they navigate various departments and services within the hospital. They ensure that each transition—from admission through to discharge and even post-discharge care—is handled smoothly.
- **Coordination of Care Transitions**: Case managers coordinate with various specialists to manage the logistics of patient care transitions. This includes organizing transfers between departments, such as from surgery to recovery units, and facilitating discharge planning to ensure patients receive appropriate follow-up care, whether at home or in another care facility.

Challenges and Solutions in Service Integration

- **Challenges**: Despite the best mechanisms, service integration can face challenges such as information silos, variations in care practices, and resistance to change among staff.
- **Solutions**: Hospitals address these challenges by investing in robust IT solutions, continuous staff training, and fostering a culture of collaboration and openness. Regular feedback mechanisms and quality improvement initiatives also support the ongoing refinement of integration strategies.

The mechanisms of service integration in hospitals are foundational to ensuring that patient care is efficient, effective, and patient-centered.

Through sophisticated communication systems, collaborative care teams, standardized clinical pathways, and dedicated case management, hospitals strive to create an environment where services are seamlessly integrated. This holistic approach not only improves patient outcomes but also enhances the satisfaction of both patients and healthcare providers, ultimately contributing to the operational excellence of healthcare institutions. As healthcare continues to evolve, the importance of effective service integration remains paramount, driving continuous improvement in hospital operations and patient care services.

Examples of Integrated Services

Effective service integration in hospitals ensures that patient care is seamless and comprehensive, spanning multiple departments and specialties. This section explores specific examples of how integrated services operate within hospital systems, focusing on the coordination between different departments to provide a continuum of care for patients with varying medical needs.

Emergency and Trauma Services to Intensive Care Integration

- **Seamless Patient Transitions**: The transition from the Emergency Department (ED) to the Intensive Care Unit (ICU) is one of the most critical pathways in hospital care. Patients who suffer from severe injuries or acute medical conditions require immediate and continuous care, making the smooth transition between these units vital.

- **Protocols and Procedures**: Hospitals employ specific protocols to ensure that when a patient is transferred from the ED to the ICU, all necessary medical information follows them without delay. This includes details of any interventions already performed, medications administered, and the patient's response to initial treatments.

- **Continuity of Care**: This integration ensures that the high level of monitoring and treatment initiated in the ED is continued in the ICU without interruption, providing patients with the best possible chance of recovery.

Oncology and Palliative Care Integration

- **Holistic Approach to Cancer Care**: Integration between oncology and palliative care teams addresses both the curative and comfort aspects of cancer treatment. While oncologists focus on treating the cancer itself, palliative care specialists concentrate on managing symptoms and improving the quality of life for patients, both during and after treatment.

- **Early Integration Benefits**: Incorporating palliative care early in the cancer treatment process has been shown to enhance patient outcomes, reduce depression, and in some cases, extend survival. This integrated approach ensures that patients receive comprehensive support that addresses physical, emotional, and spiritual needs.

- **Communication and Coordination**: Regular meetings between oncology and palliative care teams help maintain a unified approach to patient care, ensuring that all team members are updated on the patient's condition and treatment preferences.

Maternal and Neonatal Services Integration

- **Managing High-Risk Pregnancies and Births**: The collaboration between obstetrics and neonatology is crucial, especially for high-risk pregnancies where complications are anticipated. This integration ensures that immediately upon birth, newborns receive specialized care if needed, directly within the neonatal intensive care unit (NICU).

- **Continuum of Care**: From prenatal visits in the obstetrics department through to delivery and postnatal care, integration ensures that maternal and neonatal health professionals work together to monitor and manage the health of both mother and baby. This collaborative approach allows for immediate intervention by neonatal specialists during and after delivery, which is essential for premature or at-risk infants.

- **Educational and Support Services**: Integrated services also include education for expecting parents about what to expect during delivery and post-delivery, particularly if their child will need NICU care. This helps in preparing parents for potential scenarios, reducing anxiety, and fostering parental involvement.

These examples of integrated services within hospitals demonstrate the importance of coordinated care across different medical specialties and departments. By ensuring seamless transitions, continuous communication, and collaborative treatment planning, hospitals can provide patient-centric care that addresses complex medical needs effectively. This holistic approach not only improves patient outcomes but also enhances the overall efficiency of hospital operations, showcasing the profound impact of integrated healthcare services on patient care quality.

Challenges and Solutions in Service Integration

Effective service integration is critical for seamless hospital operations and high-quality patient care. However, achieving this integration can be fraught with challenges stemming from various systemic, cultural, and technological barriers. Understanding these challenges and exploring potential solutions is essential for improving hospital efficiency and patient outcomes.

Challenges in Service Integration

1. **Departmental Silos**: Hospitals often operate in departmental silos where each unit functions independently with its processes and management styles. This can lead to a lack of coordination and communication across departments, which is detrimental to providing integrated care.

2. **Operational Cultural Differences**: Different departments may have distinct cultures and ways of working, which can lead to misunderstandings and conflicts. For instance, the fast-paced decision-making style in emergency departments might clash with the more deliberate pace in departments like dermatology or reconstructive surgery.

3. **Technological Limitations**: Inadequate or outdated technology can severely hinder the sharing of information and real-time communication across departments. Systems that are not interoperable cannot exchange information seamlessly, which leads to gaps in patient data and potentially compromises patient care.

4. **Communication Gaps**: Without a standardized communication protocol, important patient information may be lost between shifts or during transfers between departments, leading to errors and inefficiencies that could affect patient outcomes.

Solutions to Enhance Service Integration

1. **Implementing Interprofessional Education Programs**:
2. **Purpose**: To cultivate a culture of collaboration and mutual respect among different healthcare professionals.
3. **Implementation**: Through workshops, joint training sessions, and simulation exercises, staff from various departments can learn about each other's roles, constraints, and contributions to patient care.
4. **Investing in Advanced IT Infrastructure**:
5. **Integrated Health Information Systems**: Implementing or upgrading to state-of-the-art health information systems that support EHR interoperability across departments can significantly improve data sharing.
6. **Benefits**: Enhances the accuracy and availability of patient information, reducing errors and allowing for more informed decision-making.
7. **Developing Standardized Communication Protocols**:
8. **Clinical Handoff Tools**: Tools like SBAR (Situation, Background, Assessment, Recommendation) provide a standardized framework for communication that can be used across different departments.
9. **Impact**: Such tools ensure that critical patient information is conveyed consistently and comprehensively, which is vital during transitions in care.
10. **Creating Integrated Care Teams**:
11. **Multidisciplinary Teams**: Form teams that include professionals from various specialties to manage complex cases, ensuring that all aspects of a patient's care are considered.
12. **Regular Coordination Meetings**: Scheduled meetings can help maintain open lines of communication and facilitate ongoing care management discussions.

. . .

Service integration within hospitals faces significant challenges, but with thoughtful strategies and investments, these can be effectively addressed. By fostering interprofessional education, upgrading technological infrastructure, standardizing communication, and promoting teamwork, hospitals can overcome barriers to integration. Such efforts not only enhance the efficiency of hospital operations but also significantly improve the quality of care that patients receive, reflecting a holistic approach to healthcare delivery.

The integration of services within hospitals is a cornerstone of modern healthcare delivery, ensuring that care is not only comprehensive but also cohesive across various stages of treatment. This chapter's exploration into how hospital departments collaborate and share information sheds light on the operational excellence necessary for high-quality healthcare. Understanding these integration mechanisms helps healthcare professionals navigate the complexities of hospital operations and contributes to their ability to provide patient-centered care. As healthcare continues to evolve, so too will the strategies for optimizing service integration, underscoring the need for continuous improvement in systems and processes within hospital settings.

In-Depth Exploration of Operational Challenges and Solutions in Hospital Management

The effective management of hospital departments is a complex endeavor that involves navigating numerous operational challenges. These challenges range from resource allocation and staffing to the efficient use of technology and process optimization. Addressing these issues is crucial for maintaining smooth hospital operations and ensuring the delivery of high-quality patient care. This section will explore the common operational challenges faced by hospitals and discuss innovative solutions and management practices that help overcome these obstacles.

Common Operational Challenges in Hospital Management

Managing a hospital involves navigating a complex array of operational challenges that can affect every aspect of healthcare delivery. From resource allocation to compliance with regulations, hospital administrators must continuously strive to optimize operations while maintaining the highest standards of patient care. This section explores the prevalent challenges faced by hospital management and discusses strategies to address them effectively.

Resource Allocation

- **Challenges in Resource Management**: Hospitals operate with finite resources, which include not only financial budgets but also medical supplies and human resources. Effective allocation of these resources is crucial to prevent wastage and ensure that there are no shortages that could impact patient care.
- **Strategies for Effective Allocation**: Implementing sophisticated resource management systems can help administrators forecast demand and plan resource allocation more accurately. Utilizing data analytics to monitor resource usage trends and predict future needs can also optimize resource use.

Staffing Challenges

- **Ensuring Adequate Staffing**: Hospitals face the constant challenge of having enough qualified staff to cover all operational needs, especially during peak times and in the face of unexpected staff absences.

- **Addressing Staffing Issues**: Adopting flexible staffing solutions such as per diem staff or float pools can help manage short-term absences without overburdening existing staff. Investing in staff development and retention strategies, such as competitive salaries, career development opportunities, and a supportive work environment, can also help maintain a stable workforce.

Technology Integration

- **Keeping Up with Advancements**: As medical technology advances rapidly, integrating these new tools into existing hospital operations presents significant challenges. The technology must be compatible with existing systems and staff need to be trained to use new tools effectively.
- **Strategies for Technology Integration**: Developing a comprehensive technology integration plan is essential. This should include a phased rollout of new technologies, comprehensive training programs for staff, and ongoing support and maintenance. Collaborations with technology providers can also provide additional support for integration.

Regulatory Compliance

- **Navigating Complex Regulations**: Hospitals must adhere to a wide range of health and safety regulations, which can vary significantly between different jurisdictions. Compliance is crucial not only to avoid financial penalties but also to ensure the safety and well-being of patients.
- **Ensuring Compliance**: Establishing a dedicated compliance department within the hospital can help stay

on top of regulatory changes and ensure that all practices are in accordance with the latest laws and standards. Regular training sessions for staff on regulatory compliance and best practices are also vital.

Managing a hospital involves addressing multiple complex challenges that can impact the efficiency of operations and the quality of patient care. By effectively managing resources, ensuring adequate staffing, integrating new technologies seamlessly, and maintaining strict compliance with regulations, hospitals can overcome these challenges. These efforts require careful planning, strategic investment, and continuous improvement in operational practices. With these strategies in place, hospitals can not only meet the current needs of their patients and staff but also prepare for future challenges in an ever-evolving healthcare landscape.

Innovative Solutions and Management Practices

As healthcare environments grow increasingly complex, hospitals are constantly seeking innovative solutions to enhance operational efficiency, improve patient care, and optimize resource utilization. This section outlines several cutting-edge management practices and technologies that are being implemented in hospitals to address these challenges.

Advanced Resource Management Systems

- **Implementation and Benefits**: Sophisticated resource management systems use advanced algorithms to analyze past usage patterns and predict future demand for services. By accurately forecasting needs, hospitals can better allocate resources like staffing, medical supplies, and bed availability.

- **Impact on Hospital Efficiency**: These systems help in minimizing waste and ensuring that resources are available where and when they are needed, thereby improving overall hospital efficiency and patient satisfaction.

Flexible Staffing Models

- **Types of Flexible Staffing**: To handle fluctuations in patient volume without excessive strain on permanent staff, hospitals are adopting flexible staffing models. Float pools and per diem staff arrangements allow hospitals to have additional personnel available when needed without the costs associated with full-time employees.
- **Benefits to Employee Well-being**: These models not only help manage unexpected spikes in demand but also contribute to better work-life balance for staff, reducing burnout and improving job satisfaction.

Telemedicine and Remote Monitoring

- **Expanding Care Delivery**: Telemedicine and remote patient monitoring have revolutionized how care is delivered, particularly in reaching patients in remote areas or those unable to visit hospitals frequently.
- **Reduction in Resource Strain**: By reducing the number of in-person visits, these technologies help conserve hospital resources and reduce the burden on facility-based services. Additionally, they provide continuous monitoring and real-time data to healthcare providers, enhancing the ability to make informed treatment decisions.

Process Optimization through Lean Management

- **Lean Management in Healthcare**: Lean management principles, originally developed in manufacturing, are now being adapted for healthcare settings. These principles focus on value creation for the patient by identifying and eliminating non-value-added activities.
- **Outcomes of Lean Implementation**: Hospitals implementing lean management report significant improvements in patient flow, reduced wait times, lower costs, and enhanced patient care outcomes. Continuous improvement cycles also foster an environment of innovation and efficiency.

Continuous Professional Development and Training

- **Ongoing Education**: Continuous training programs are essential for keeping hospital staff up-to-date with the latest medical technologies, healthcare practices, and regulatory changes.
- **Impact on Care Quality**: Regular professional development ensures that all team members are proficient in using new tools and understanding new procedures, which directly enhances the quality of care provided to patients.

Adopting innovative solutions and management practices is crucial for hospitals aiming to enhance service delivery and operational efficiency. From advanced resource management and flexible staffing to the integration of telemedicine and lean processes, these strategies are vital in adapting to the dynamic healthcare landscape. As hospitals continue to evolve, the implementation of these innovative practices will be key to sustaining improvements and ensuring high standards of patient care.

Chapter 6 has provided an in-depth exploration of the various hospital departments and services, highlighting the complexities and critical nature of effective hospital management. By understanding the functions, services, and coordination efforts required across different departments, this chapter has shed light on the foundational aspects of hospital operations that ensure patient care is both effective and efficient.

The challenges faced by hospital management, such as resource allocation, staffing, technology integration, and regulatory compliance, are substantial yet surmountable with the right strategies. Innovative solutions such as advanced resource management systems, flexible staffing models, telemedicine, and lean management practices have been discussed as key to enhancing operational efficiency. These practices not only streamline hospital operations but also significantly improve the quality of patient care.

As the healthcare landscape evolves with advancements in medicine and technology, the adaptability and responsiveness of hospital management strategies are increasingly critical. This chapter has illustrated how embracing innovation and effective management can prepare hospital systems to meet current and future challenges, ensuring the continued delivery of high-quality healthcare.

Transitioning from the broad overview of hospital operations and challenges in Chapter 6, we now turn our focus to a more granular aspect of healthcare that is pivotal to all functions within a hospital—Everyday Medical Terminology. Chapter 7 will delve into the specific language and terms that are used daily in the healthcare environment. This chapter aims to equip healthcare professionals and students alike with a thorough understanding of medical terminology, enhancing communication clarity and ensuring precision in patient care.

Medical terminology serves as the language through which professionals communicate about diseases, treatments, and patient conditions. A comprehensive grasp of this terminology is not just beneficial but essential for effective communication among healthcare providers and between providers and patients. By breaking down complex terms and explaining their origins and meanings, Chapter 7 will provide the tools necessary for healthcare professionals to engage more effectively in their roles, whether they are diagnosing conditions, explaining procedures to patients, or documenting care activities.

In summary, as we move from the macro perspectives of hospital management to the micro details of medical language in Chapter 7, we continue to build on the foundational knowledge necessary for excellence in healthcare delivery. This next chapter will serve as both an educational resource and a practical guide for navigating the everyday language used in the healthcare sector.

Introduction to Chapter 7: Everyday Medical Terminology

Chapter 7 is dedicated to "Everyday Medical Terminology," a vital component of communication within healthcare settings. This chapter delves into the critical aspects of medical language that ensure clarity, efficiency, and precision, crucial for the fast-paced environment of healthcare. By understanding and mastering these elements, healthcare professionals and students can ensure effective communication, accurate documentation, and enhance overall patient care.

Understanding Medical Terminology

Medical terminology allows healthcare professionals to quickly convey complex information, document patient interactions effectively, and collaborate efficiently across different specialties. This chapter is structured into two significant sections:

1. **Common Medical Abbreviations**: This section provides an exhaustive list of abbreviations commonly used in medical documentation, prescriptions, and communications. You will learn each abbreviation's meaning, usage, and context, enhancing your ability to communicate with precision and avoid potential misunderstandings that could impact patient care.

2. **Medical Slang and Jargon**: The informal language used among healthcare professionals often appears in everyday conversations within hospitals and clinics. This part of the chapter explores these terms, providing insights into how they can simplify communication but also highlighting the caution needed to prevent misinterpretation.

The Role of Medical Terminology in Healthcare

Proficiency in both formal abbreviations and the nuances of medical slang is essential for any healthcare professional for several reasons:

- **Enhanced Communication**: Effective use of medical terminology is crucial for clear and concise communication with colleagues and patients, ensuring mutual understanding of treatments, procedures, and health conditions.

- **Improved Documentation**: Accurate documentation is vital for maintaining patient records, complying with legal standards, and facilitating communication with insurance providers. Mastery of medical terminology is directly linked to the quality and reliability of these documents.

- **Patient Safety**: Correct application of medical terminology significantly affects patient safety, helping to prevent medication errors, misdiagnoses, and inappropriate treatments.

This chapter includes exercises and real-life scenarios to help you practice and apply medical terminology in practical settings. These interactive elements are designed to reinforce learning and ensure you are well-prepared to use this knowledge effectively in your daily professional activities.

Upon completing Chapter 7, you will possess a robust understanding of medical terminology essential for your career and role in providing high-quality healthcare. This knowledge will serve as a cornerstone of your professional development, bridging the gap between theoretical learning and practical application in the healthcare field.

Introduction to Medical Terminology

Medical terminology is the specialized language used by healthcare professionals to ensure precise and efficient communication. It is critical for documenting medical records, conducting medical research, and delivering patient care. This section aims to provide a thorough understanding of the structure, function, and application of medical terminology, equipping healthcare students and professionals with the skills necessary to navigate complex medical conversations and documentation effectively.

Structure of Medical Terminology

Understanding the structure of medical terminology is essential for healthcare professionals and students as it forms the foundation of precise communication within the medical field. This section explores the fundamental components of medical terms: root words, prefixes, suffixes, and combining forms, providing a systematic approach to decoding and using medical language effectively.

Root Words, Prefixes, and Suffixes

1. **Root Words**: The root of a medical term usually indicates the involved body part or the primary concept. For example, 'nephro' refers to the kidneys, and 'gastr' refers to the stomach. These roots are derived predominantly from Latin and Greek languages, giving a universal basis for the medical terminology used globally.

2. **Prefixes**: Prefixes are added to the beginning of root words to modify their meaning by providing additional context. They can describe location, time, number, or condition. For example:

3. 'Hyper-' signifies above or excessive; hyperactive means overly active.

4. 'Sub-' means under or below; subcutaneous means situated or applied under the skin.

5. **Suffixes**: Suffixes are attached to the end of root words to indicate the type of procedure, condition, disease, or part of speech. They often dictate the medical context of the term, such as:

6. '-itis' indicates inflammation, as in arthritis (inflammation of the joints).

7. '-ectomy' denotes surgical removal, as in appendectomy (surgical removal of the appendix).

Combining Forms

1. **Purpose of Combining Forms**: Combining forms enhance the clarity and pronunciation of medical terms, especially when multiple root words are involved or when the term would be awkward to pronounce without them.

2. **Structure**: A combining form is created when a root word is combined with a vowel—usually 'o', but sometimes 'a' or 'i'—that does not add significantly to the

term's meaning but aids in its pronunciation and the addition of suffixes. For example:

3. 'Osteoarthritis' combines 'osteo-' (bone) and 'arthritis' (joint inflammation) to describe inflammation that involves bone and joint.

Examples and Usage

- **Cardiology**: From 'cardio-' (heart) and '-logy' (study of), referring to the study of heart functions and disorders.
- **Hematology**: From 'hemato-' (blood) and '-logy', indicating the study of blood and its diseases.
- **Neurology**: Combines 'neuro-' (nerve) with '-logy', referring to the study of the nervous system and its disorders.
- **Dermatology**: From 'dermato-' (skin) and '-logy' (study of), referring to the study of skin and its disorders.
- **Gastroenterology**: From 'gastro-' (stomach), 'entero-' (intestine), and '-logy', indicating the study of the digestive system.
- **Ophthalmology**: From 'ophthalmo-' (eye) and '-logy', referring to the study of the eye and its disorders.
- **Oncology**: From 'onco-' (tumor) and '-logy', indicating the study of tumors and cancer.
- **Pathology**: From 'patho-' (disease) and '-logy', referring to the study of diseases and their processes.
- **Psychology**: From 'psycho-' (mind) and '-logy', indicating the study of the mind and behavior.
- **Rheumatology**: From 'rheumato-' (flow, flux) and '-logy', referring to the study of rheumatic diseases like arthritis.
- **Nephrology**: From 'nephro-' (kidney) and '-logy', indicating the study of kidney function and kidney-related diseases.

- **Endocrinology**: From 'endocrino-' (endocrine glands) and '-logy', referring to the study of the endocrine system and hormonal disorders.
- **Pulmonology**: From 'pulmono-' (lungs) and '-logy', referring to the study of the respiratory system.
- **Urology**: From 'uro-' (urine, urinary system) and '-logy', indicating the study of the urinary tract and male reproductive organs.
- **Orthopedics**: From 'ortho-' (straight) and '-pedics' (related to children), originally referring to the study of correcting deformities in children, now more broadly related to the musculoskeletal system.
- **Pediatrics**: From 'ped-' (child) and '-iatrics' (medical treatment), referring to the medical treatment of infants and children.
- **Gerontology**: From 'geronto-' (old age) and '-logy', indicating the study of aging and the elderly.
- **Hepatology**: From 'hepato-' (liver) and '-logy', referring to the study of the liver, gallbladder, biliary tree, and pancreas.
- **Immunology**: From 'immuno-' (immune) and '-logy', indicating the study of the immune system and immune responses.
- **Toxicology**: From 'toxico-' (poison) and '-logy', referring to the study of toxins and their effects on the body.
- **Pharmacology**: From 'pharmaco-' (drugs) and '-logy', indicating the study of drugs and their effects on living organisms.
- **Radiology**: From 'radio-' (radiation) and '-logy', referring to the use of radiation for diagnosing and treating diseases.
- **Gynecology**: From 'gyneco-' (woman) and '-logy', indicating the study of the female reproductive system.

Practical Applications of Medical Terminology
Medical Documentation

1. **Clarity and Precision**: The use of correct medical terminology in documentation is vital for maintaining clear and precise patient records. This ensures that any healthcare provider reviewing the records—whether a doctor, nurse, or specialist—can quickly understand the patient's medical history, current condition, and the treatments they have received.

2. **Legal and Compliance Relevance**: Accurate medical documentation is also critical for legal protection and compliance with healthcare regulations. Medical records serve as a legal document that can be used in court, making the accuracy and clarity of the terminology used crucial.

3. **Interdepartmental Communication**: Within hospitals, clear documentation using standard medical terminology facilitates better communication across different departments. For example, if a patient is transferred from surgery to post-operative care, the medical terms used in their records help provide a seamless transition and continuity of care.

4. **Data Analysis and Research**: Medical records documented using standardized terminology are easier to analyze for research and quality improvement purposes. This standardization allows researchers and healthcare administrators to track health outcomes and identify trends or issues in patient care.

Patient Communication

1. **Enhancing Understanding**: Proper use of medical terminology helps healthcare professionals explain

complex diagnoses and treatment plans to patients in a way that is easier to understand. This transparency is crucial for building trust and ensuring that patients are well-informed about their health conditions.

2. **Improving Compliance**: When patients fully understand their diagnoses and the reasons behind specific treatment plans, they are more likely to comply with the recommendations provided. For instance, explaining the term 'hypertension' as high blood pressure and detailing its risks can motivate patients to adhere to prescribed medication regimes and lifestyle changes.

3. **Supporting Patient Education**: Effective use of medical terminology extends to patient education materials, such as brochures, websites, and instructional videos. Clear and correct terminology helps ensure that these materials are both informative and accessible, aiding patients in learning more about their health conditions and how to manage them.

4. **Cultural Sensitivity and Personalization**: Tailoring the use of medical terminology based on the patient's level of understanding and cultural background is also important. This personalized approach helps in making the communication more patient-centric, thereby enhancing the overall patient experience in the healthcare system.

5. **Facilitating Shared Decision Making**: Knowledgeable use of medical terminology empowers patients to engage more actively in their healthcare decisions. This shared decision-making process relies on clear communication and mutual understanding, fostered through the correct and effective use of medical language.

The structure of medical terminology, with its roots, prefixes, suffixes, and combining forms, provides a systematic and standardized way to describe complex medical concepts succinctly and accurately. Mastery of this language is not only crucial for effective communication among healthcare professionals but also enhances the clarity of interactions with patients, ensuring a high standard of care and patient education. This foundational knowledge sets the stage for further exploration of specific medical terms and their applications across various medical specialties.

Function of Medical Terminology

Medical terminology is not merely a formalized set of terms; it serves as the backbone of all communication within healthcare settings. Its primary function is to enable precision, efficiency, and clarity in the transmission of medical information. This exploration delves into how medical terminology serves these vital functions and why it is indispensable in healthcare.

Clear Communication

- **Standardization Across Professionals**: Medical terminology creates a standardized language that transcends individual dialects or colloquialisms, allowing healthcare professionals worldwide to understand each other clearly. This is crucial in settings where multidisciplinary teams collaborate on patient care.

- **Preventing Misinterpretations**: Precise terminology reduces the likelihood of errors in patient care by preventing misunderstandings. For example, the specific terms used to describe medication dosages, surgical procedures, and diagnoses leave little room for the ambiguities that might arise from everyday language.

- **Case Studies and Real-World Examples**: For instance, the distinction between 'hypertrophy' (increase in the size of an organ or tissue through the enlargement of cells) and 'hyperplasia' (increase in the number of cells) can significantly alter treatment plans and expected outcomes.

Efficient Documentation

- **Streamlining Record-Keeping**: In the digitized environment of modern healthcare, having standardized medical terminology helps in the organization and retrieval of patient information. This standardization supports electronic health record (EHR) systems which are pivotal in maintaining longitudinal patient records.
- **Facilitating Faster Care Delivery**: Efficient documentation means that healthcare providers can quickly review a patient's history and make informed decisions without delay—critical in high-stakes environments like emergency rooms or intensive care units.
- **Impact on Healthcare Costs**: Reducing the time spent on administrative tasks through streamlined documentation directly impacts the cost-effectiveness of healthcare delivery, allowing more resources to be directed towards patient care.

Enhancing Clinical Efficiency

- **Rapid Exchange in Critical Situations**: In emergency situations, the ability to communicate quickly and clearly can be life-saving. Medical terminology enables this by condensing complex information into concise terms that convey the necessary details without ambiguity.
- **Training and Simulations**: Effective training in medical terminology helps simulate real-life emergencies, where every second count, and clear communication is

key to successful outcomes. These simulations often use scenarios like cardiac arrests (described medically as 'myocardial infarctions') to train personnel in responding effectively.

- **Interdisciplinary Coordination**: In hospitals, the coordination between various specialties—such as when a patient with a cardiac issue (cardiology) needs surgery (surgical team) and post-operative care (rehabilitation)—relies heavily on clear, precise language to describe patient conditions and prescribed treatments.

The function of medical terminology extends beyond simple communication; it is a critical component that underpins all aspects of healthcare. By enabling clear communication, efficient documentation, and enhancing clinical efficiency, medical terminology ensures that healthcare systems can operate smoothly and effectively, providing safe and timely care to patients. As healthcare continues to evolve, the role of medical terminology in supporting new technologies and interdisciplinary approaches will undoubtedly expand, further underscoring its importance in the medical field.

Application of Medical Terminology

Medical terminology is more than just a linguistic tool; it is integral to various aspects of healthcare, from diagnosis and treatment to education and communication. This section explores the critical applications of medical terminology in clinical settings, illustrating how its precise use impacts the effectiveness of healthcare delivery.

Diagnostic Processes

- **Precision in Diagnosis**: Accurate diagnosis starts with the correct interpretation and use of medical terminology. For instance, distinguishing between 'myocardial infarction' (a heart attack due to blood flow blockage) and 'cardiac arrest' (sudden loss of heart function) is crucial as each condition requires different immediate responses and treatments.

- **Clinical Decision-Making**: Understanding and using the correct medical terms enhance the decision-making process, allowing healthcare providers to quickly and effectively determine the appropriate course of action based on diagnoses.

- **Communication Among Specialists**: When specialists are involved in a patient's care, precise terminology ensures that all parties have a clear understanding of the diagnosis. This is particularly important in multi-disciplinary team meetings where complex cases are discussed.

Treatment and Procedures

- **Clarity in Treatment Plans**: Medical terminology specifies treatment protocols in a universally understood language among healthcare professionals. For instance, a 'laparotomy', which is the surgical opening of the abdomen, clearly communicates the nature and invasiveness of the procedure to all involved in the patient's care.

- **Informed Consent**: Before undergoing any procedure, patients must be fully informed about what the procedure entails. Clear explanations using correct medical terminology help patients understand the risks, benefits, and alternatives available, facilitating informed consent.

- **Documentation and Record-Keeping**: Accurate use of medical terminology in documenting treatment plans and surgical procedures ensures that patient records are precise and comprehensive. This documentation is crucial for follow-up care, audits, and legal purposes.

Educational Purposes

- **Training Healthcare Professionals**: For students and trainees entering medical fields, proficiency in medical terminology is essential. It forms the foundation of their medical education, from anatomy and physiology to pathology and pharmacology.
- **Continuing Professional Development**: Ongoing education and training in new medical terminology and procedures are critical for healthcare professionals to stay current with the latest advances in medicine. This continuous learning is often facilitated through professional courses and seminars where medical terminology forms the core content.
- **Public Education and Outreach**: Healthcare professionals often use medical terminology in public health education. Simplifying complex medical terms for community health talks, pamphlets, and preventive care guidelines helps bridge the knowledge gap and promote public health literacy.

The application of medical terminology extends across all domains of healthcare, making it a vital element of clinical practice. Its role in diagnostics, treatment planning, and medical education underscores its importance in achieving high standards of patient care and safety. As medicine continues to evolve, the precise and informed use of medical terminology will remain fundamental in training future generations of healthcare providers and enhancing patient outcomes in the ever-changing landscape of healthcare.

Teaching Medical Terminology

Teaching medical terminology effectively is crucial in preparing students and healthcare professionals to excel in the medical field. This section examines how various educational strategies can enhance the understanding and retention of medical terminology, which is essential for clear communication and effective practice in healthcare settings.

Interactive Learning Methods

- **Diversity in Teaching Tools**: Engaging students through diverse learning tools like flashcards, quizzes, and interactive software makes the learning process more dynamic and less monotonous. These tools cater to different learning styles—visual, auditory, and kinesthetic—enhancing the ability to memorize and recall complex medical terms.
- **Use of Flashcards**: Flashcards are particularly useful for breaking down complex terms into manageable components, such as prefixes, suffixes, and root words, facilitating easier understanding and long-term retention.
- **Digital and Interactive Software**: Modern educational technology offers interactive platforms that simulate medical scenarios or provide virtual dissections, which can help students visualize and apply medical terminology in context.

Clinical Scenario Simulations

- **Real-World Application**: Clinical scenario simulations are vital for applying theoretical knowledge in practical settings. These simulations involve role-playing or using mannequins in a controlled environment to enact medical situations where specific terminology is used actively.

- **Enhancing Clinical Decision-Making**: By practicing in simulations that mimic real-life medical conditions, students and new professionals can learn how to quickly and accurately use medical terminology in diagnosing and treating patients. For example, a simulation might involve a staged setup of an acute myocardial infarction where participants must communicate effectively using correct medical terms to manage the patient.

- **Feedback and Improvement**: Simulations often provide immediate feedback, a crucial element in educational settings, which helps learners correct mistakes, understand concepts more deeply, and refine their professional skills. Continuous feedback helps bridge the gap between theoretical knowledge and practical application.

Chapter 6
Mastering Medical Terminology

Teaching medical terminology through interactive methods and clinical scenario simulations offers a comprehensive approach that significantly enhances learning outcomes. These methods not only help in retaining complex medical terms but also ensure that learners can apply their knowledge effectively in real-world healthcare settings. As the healthcare industry continues to evolve, the methodologies for teaching medical terminology will also need to adapt, incorporating new technologies and learning platforms to meet the changing demands of healthcare education. Ultimately, the goal is to equip healthcare professionals with the linguistic tools they need to succeed in their careers and provide the highest level of care to their patients.

By mastering medical terminology, healthcare professionals and students can enhance their ability to communicate effectively within the medical community and with their patients. This chapter provides the tools and knowledge necessary to understand and use medical terminology accurately in everyday clinical practice.

As we move forward, the next sections will build on this foundation by exploring common medical abbreviations and the informal slang and jargon used in healthcare settings, further rounding out the linguistic competence of healthcare professionals.

Common Medical Abbreviations:

Medical abbreviations are a fundamental part of healthcare communication, used extensively in medical documentation, prescriptions, and verbal communications among healthcare providers. These abbreviations streamline processes and ensure efficient and concise communication. However, their misuse can lead to significant risks, making a deep understanding of these abbreviations essential for any healthcare professional.

Importance of Medical Abbreviations

- **Efficiency and Speed**: In fast-paced healthcare environments, such as emergency rooms or intensive care units, the use of abbreviations can save valuable time.
- **Standardization of Communication**: Across different healthcare settings, standardized abbreviations help maintain clarity and consistency in medical records, ensuring that care is safely and effectively communicated and administered.

Comprehensive List of 100 Common Medical Abbreviations

1. **ABG** - Arterial Blood Gas
2. **BID** - Twice Daily
3. **BP** - Blood Pressure
4. **BPM** - Beats Per Minute
5. **CXR** - Chest X-Ray
6. **DNR** - Do Not Resuscitate
7. **DOB** - Date of Birth
8. **ED** - Emergency Department
9. **ENT** - Ear, Nose, and Throat
10. **FBS** - Fasting Blood Sugar

11. **GFR** - Glomerular Filtration Rate
12. **HbA1c** - Hemoglobin A1c
13. **ICU** - Intensive Care Unit
14. **IV** - Intravenous
15. **KUB** - Kidney, Ureter, and Bladder
16. **LFT** - Liver Function Test
17. **MI** - Myocardial Infarction
18. **MRI** - Magnetic Resonance Imaging
19. **NPO** - Nothing by Mouth (nil per os)
20. **OR** - Operating Room
21. **OTC** - Over The Counter
22. **PCN** - Penicillin
23. **PRN** - As Needed (pro re nata)
24. **PT** - Physical Therapy/Prothrombin Time
25. **PTSD** - Post-Traumatic Stress Disorder
26. **QID** - Four Times a Day
27. **RBC** - Red Blood Cell
28. **ROM** - Range of Motion
29. **Rx** - Prescription
30. **SOB** - Shortness of Breath
31. **TIA** - Transient Ischemic Attack
32. **TID** - Three Times a Day
33. **UA** - Urinalysis
34. **UTI** - Urinary Tract Infection
35. **VS** - Vital Signs
36. **WBC** - White Blood Cell
37. **XRT** - Radiation Therapy
38. **y/o** - Years Old
39. **HCT** - Hematocrit
40. **HDL** - High-Density Lipoprotein
41. **HR** - Heart Rate
42. **HS** - At Bedtime (hora somni)
43. **I&D** - Incision and Drainage
44. **IM** - Intramuscular

45. **INR** - International Normalized Ratio
46. **LDL** - Low-Density Lipoprotein
47. **LOC** - Level of Consciousness
48. **NGT** - Nasogastric Tube
49. **O2** - Oxygen
50. **PE** - Pulmonary Embolism / Physical Exa
51. **AAA** - Abdominal Aortic Aneurysm
52. **AFB** - Acid-Fast Bacillus
53. **ALT** - Alanine Aminotransferase
54. **AMA** - Against Medical Advice
55. **APS** - Antiphospholipid Syndrome
56. **AV** - Atrioventricular
57. **BBB** - Bundle Branch Block
58. **BC** - Birth Control
59. **BKA** - Below Knee Amputation
60. **BMP** - Basic Metabolic Panel
61. **BPH** - Benign Prostatic Hyperplasia
62. **BSI** - Blood Stream Infection
63. **CABG** - Coronary Artery Bypass Graft
64. **CAD** - Coronary Artery Disease
65. **CBC** - Complete Blood Count
66. **CF** - Cystic Fibrosis
67. **CKD** - Chronic Kidney Disease
68. **CML** - Chronic Myeloid Leukemia
69. **CNS** - Central Nervous System
70. **COPD** - Chronic Obstructive Pulmonary Disease
71. **CPAP** - Continuous Positive Airway Pressure
72. **CPR** - Cardiopulmonary Resuscitation
73. **CPT** - Current Procedural Terminology
74. **CRP** - C-Reactive Protein
75. **CSF** - Cerebrospinal Fluid
76. **CTA** - Clear to Auscultation
77. **DVT** - Deep Vein Thrombosis
78. **EBV** - Epstein-Barr Virus

79. **ECG** - Electrocardiogram
80. **EEG** - Electroencephalogram
81. **EKG** - Electrocardiogram
82. **ELISA** - Enzyme-Linked Immunosorbent Assay
83. **EMG** - Electromyogram
84. **ENT** - Ear, Nose, and Throat
85. **ESR** - Erythrocyte Sedimentation Rate
86. **FHR** - Fetal Heart Rate
87. **FVC** - Forced Vital Capacity
88. **GAD** - Generalized Anxiety Disorder
89. **GERD** - Gastroesophageal Reflux Disease
90. **GTT** - Glucose Tolerance Test
91. **HCG** - Human Chorionic Gonadotropin
92. **HDL** - High-Density Lipoprotein
93. **HIV** - Human Immunodeficiency Virus
94. **HRT** - Hormone Replacement Therapy
95. **IBD** - Inflammatory Bowel Disease
96. **IBS** - Irritable Bowel Syndrome
97. **ICD** - Implantable Cardioverter-Defibrillator
98. **IDDM** - Insulin-Dependent Diabetes Mellitus
99. **IFA** - Indirect Fluorescent Antibody
100. **IGRA** - Interferon Gamma Release Assay

Understanding and correctly using medical abbreviations is crucial for all healthcare professionals. Each abbreviation listed plays a significant role in facilitating efficient communication. However, it is essential to use them appropriately to prevent misunderstandings and ensure accurate patient care. For healthcare students and professionals, being proficient in these abbreviations is non-negotiable for safe and effective practice. This comprehensive list serves as a tool not only for quick reference but also for deepening one's understanding of the language used in daily medical practice.

· · ·

Medical Slang and Jargon:

In the bustling corridors of hospitals and clinics, medical professionals often use slang and jargon as shorthand to convey complex information efficiently. This section delves into the informal language that permeates everyday conversations within healthcare settings. While these terms can streamline communication and foster a sense of camaraderie among staff, they require careful handling to ensure clarity and prevent misunderstandings.

Understanding Medical Slang and Jargon

Medical slang and jargon are informal terms that have evolved over time within the healthcare environment. These terms often arise from a need for quick and concise communication. Here, we explore the dual nature of medical slang—its utility and its potential pitfalls:

- **Efficiency in Communication**: Medical slang allows healthcare providers to convey information swiftly and efficiently. In emergency situations or busy clinical settings, these terms can expedite communication without the need for lengthy explanations.

- **Cultural and Group Identity**: Slang can also serve as a cultural marker within the medical community, helping to strengthen bonds among medical staff and creating a shared identity that can ease the stress of high-pressure environments.

Examples of Medical Slang and Jargon

To illustrate how medical slang and jargon function in practice, here are several commonly used terms:

- **GOMER**: "Get Out of My Emergency Room" is a pejorative term for a patient who frequently visits the emergency room for chronic but non-emergency medical issues.

- **Frequent Flyer**: Refers to a patient who often returns to the hospital or clinic for treatment, implying a repeated pattern of care.
- **Code Blue**: A term widely recognized in many hospitals to indicate a patient requiring immediate resuscitation, typically from cardiac or respiratory arrest.
- **Baby Catcher**: An affectionate slang term for obstetricians or midwives.
- **Zebra**: Medical slang for a surprising, often exotic, diagnosis, derived from the saying "When you hear hoofbeats, think of horses not zebras."
- **Turf**: Refers to transferring a patient to another department or team to shift responsibility.
- **Crasher**: A patient who rapidly deteriorates and needs immediate intervention.
- **The Golden Hour**: Refers to the critical one-hour period after a traumatic injury during which treatment is most likely to prevent death.
- **Road Rash**: Abrasions from sliding on asphalt or gravel, typically associated with motorcycle or bicycle accidents.
- **Rule Out**: To eliminate a diagnosis from consideration through testing or evidence.
- **Sundowning**: Increased confusion or agitation in a patient with dementia during the late afternoon or evening.
- **Crib Death**: Another term for Sudden Infant Death Syndrome (SIDS).
- **Flea**: Slang for a pesky or annoying patient.
- **Gorked**: Refers to a patient who is unresponsive or severely brain damaged.
- **Hit the Hay**: Going to bed or ending a shift.
- **House Red**: A humorous term for blood.

Medical Terminology Study Guide

- **Incidentaloma**: An incidental finding that is not related to the current medical evaluation.
- **Jam Sandwich**: Slang for an ambulance or police car, primarily used in the UK.
- **Kiss of Life**: Refers to mouth-to-mouth resuscitation.
- **Lollipop Lesion**: A term for a tumor with a stem attachment.
- **Moonlighting**: Medical professionals working additional jobs outside of their main job, often at night.
- **Night Stick**: Night shift, or a reference to working overnight.
- **Organ Recital**: When a patient describes every ailment or complete medical history.
- **Peanut Gallery**: Group of medical students or interns observing a procedure.
- **Quack**: A derogatory term for a doctor who is considered incompetent.
- **Rabbit Hole**: Complex cases that lead to unexpected complications or diagnoses.
- **Scut Work**: Menial tasks that do not require much skill, often assigned to interns or junior staff.
- **Silver Tsunami**: The increasing proportion of elderly patients in the healthcare system.
- **Sitter**: A caregiver assigned to monitor a patient closely, often one who is at risk of harm to themselves.
- **Slow Code**: Deliberately slow response to a cardiac arrest, often in a situation where resuscitation is unlikely to succeed.
- **Status Dramaticus**: Overly dramatic patient.
- **Superuser**: A patient who frequently uses emergency services or hospital resources.
- **Swan-Ganz**: A type of catheter used for monitoring heart function.

- **Train Wreck**: A patient with multiple complex health issues.
- **Treadmill Test**: Another term for an exercise stress test.
- **Unicorn**: A case or diagnosis that is so rare it's almost mythical.
- **Vampire**: Phlebotomist or anyone who draws blood.
- **Walkie Talkie**: A patient who is ambulatory and talkative.
- **Wet Read**: Preliminary review of a radiological scan.
- **Whack**: To hit, referring usually to administering a drug.
- **Zombified**: Refers to a patient who is heavily sedated or feeling the effects of strong medication.
- **Z-Doc**: A physician who loves to prescribe sleep medication.
- **Workup**: Comprehensive medical evaluation.
- **Yankauer**: A suction tool used during surgeries.
- **X-Match**: Crossmatch test for blood transfusion compatibility.
- **Woolworth's Test**: A non-specific term for a cheap, nonspecific blood test.
- **Window Shopper**: A patient who visits multiple doctors for consultations but never follows up.
- **V-tach**: Ventricular tachycardia, a type of fast heart rate.
- **Upcoding**: Billing for a higher level of medical service than was actually provided.
- **Tube Steak**: Hospital food, generally unappetizing and bland.
- **Triage Nurse**: Nurse responsible for prioritizing patient care based on the severity of their condition.
- **Treeing**: Displaying a patient's diagnostic branches for analysis or educational purposes.

- **Tox Screen**: Toxicological screening, typically for drugs or poisons.
- **Time of Flight**: A method used in MRI scans.
- **Tick**: A derogatory term for a patient perceived as troublesome or annoying.

The Caution Needed

While medical slang can simplify communication, it carries risks that must be carefully managed:

- **Risk of Misinterpretation**: To those outside the immediate medical team or non-medical staff, such as patients and their families, these terms can be confusing or misleading, leading to misunderstandings about care and treatment.
- **Potential for Disrespect**: Some slang terms may come across as insensitive or disrespectful to patients or their conditions, potentially compromising professional integrity and patient trust.

Best Practices for Using Medical Slang and Jargon

- **Context and Audience**: Healthcare professionals should use medical slang judiciously, considering the context and the audience. Clear and professional language should be used when discussing medical care with patients or in formal medical documentation.
- **Education and Awareness**: Training healthcare professionals about the appropriate use of medical slang and its potential impact on patient care can help mitigate the risks associated with its use.

Medical slang and jargon, when used appropriately, can facilitate rapid communication among healthcare professionals. However, it is crucial to use these terms judiciously and be aware of their implications to maintain professionalism and ensure clear communication with all stakeholders in the healthcare process. This exploration serves not only as a guide to understanding and using medical slang but also as a caution to uphold the highest standards of communication within healthcare settings.

Role of Medical Terminology in Healthcare

Medical terminology is not just a technical vocabulary but a crucial tool in the infrastructure of healthcare. This exploration delves into how mastery of both formal medical abbreviations and the nuances of medical slang plays a critical role in various aspects of healthcare. Proficiency in medical terminology enhances communication, improves documentation, and increases patient safety, among other benefits.

Medical terminology facilitates precise and effective communication among healthcare professionals. This precision is particularly critical in multidisciplinary team settings where specialists from various fields collaborate to provide comprehensive patient care. For instance, in a tumor board review, clear communication using specific oncological terms helps ensure that all team members understand the treatment plans and research updates. Accurate terminology also enhances communication with patients, enabling them to understand their diagnoses and treatment options better, which is crucial for informed consent and patient involvement in healthcare decisions.

The use of standardized medical terminology is vital for creating reliable and clear medical documentation. Accurate medical records serve multiple purposes: they are legal documents, a means of communication between different healthcare providers, and a vital part of billing and insurance claims. Mastery of medical terminology ensures that health records are accurately detailed, supporting all these functions efficiently. For example, the use of the correct terms in medical records can streamline the process of insurance claims, reducing errors and delays that might otherwise occur due to misinterpretation.

The correct use of medical terminology directly impacts patient safety. In scenarios such as prescribing medication, conducting surgical procedures, or issuing medical orders, the precise use of terminology can mean the difference between correct and erroneous treatment. For example, a misunderstanding caused by incorrect terminology usage in dosing instructions can lead to a medication error, potentially harming the patient. Similarly, clear terminology in surgical consents ensures that patients and surgical teams are fully aware of the procedures being performed, thereby reducing the risk of surgical errors.

To maintain the effectiveness of medical terminology in enhancing communication, improving documentation, and ensuring patient safety, continuous education and standardization of terms are necessary. Healthcare institutions often conduct regular training sessions to ensure that all medical personnel are up-to-date with current terminology, especially as new diagnostic tools and treatments are developed. Additionally, standardizing medical terminology across different healthcare systems helps maintain consistency, especially in an increasingly globalized world where patients may receive treatment in multiple countries.

Medical terminology also plays a pivotal role in medical research and the development of new therapies. Precise terminology allows researchers to communicate complex scientific findings clearly and consistently, which is essential for advancing medical knowledge and treatment methods. Moreover, standardized medical terminology facilitates meta-analyses and systematic reviews by providing a consistent language for researchers around the world.

With the advancement of health information technology, medical terminology has integrated into electronic health records (EHRs), telemedicine, and other digital tools, enhancing the accessibility and reliability of patient information. This integration helps healthcare providers retrieve and analyze patient information more efficiently, supporting better patient outcomes.

In conclusion, the role of medical terminology in healthcare is multifaceted and indispensable. From enhancing communication among healthcare professionals to ensuring patient safety and supporting medical research, the precise use of medical terminology is foundational to the practice of modern medicine. As healthcare continues to evolve, so too will the ways in which medical terminology is applied, necessitating ongoing education and adaptation by healthcare professionals.

Overview of Everyday Medical Terminology

Chapter 7 provided an in-depth exploration of the everyday medical terminology that is pivotal for effective communication within the healthcare environment. From the precision required in medical documentation to the shorthand used in informal conversations among healthcare professionals, understanding this terminology is essential for anyone involved in patient care.

We dissected the structured aspect of medical terminology, consisting of common medical abbreviations that play a critical role in the swift and accurate transfer of information. These abbreviations help streamline communication, reduce complexity, and ensure clarity in fast-paced medical settings. This structured terminology underpins all forms of medical communication, from patient records to real-time discussions during surgical procedures.

Conversely, we delved into the more informal side of communication through medical slang and jargon. While less formal, these terms provide a quicker, often more relatable way to discuss patient conditions, treatments, and medical experiences among peers. However, the use of such language requires discretion to avoid misinterpretation or offense, maintaining professionalism and respect for patients and colleagues alike.

For students and newcomers to the medical field, mastering both formal and informal medical terminology is not just about being able to communicate. It is about integrating into the culture of healthcare, where every term or abbreviation used can significantly impact patient outcomes. Educational programs focusing on these aspects equip future healthcare providers with the tools necessary for success.

The practical applications of medical terminology in clinical settings—be it through diagnosing diseases or explaining procedures to patients—demonstrate its critical role in healthcare. Best practices were highlighted to ensure that medical professionals use terminology appropriately to support clear and effective communication.

Medical terminology is ever-evolving, with new terms, treatments, and technologies constantly emerging. Therefore, continuous learning and professional development are essential for medical professionals to keep abreast of the latest advancements and changes in the field. This ongoing education is crucial for maintaining the high standards required for patient care and medical research.

As we close this chapter, it's clear that the journey of learning and using medical terminology is continuous. For healthcare professionals, the ability to decode and utilize medical language effectively is just the beginning. The true challenge lies in applying this knowledge in real-world settings to enhance patient care, participate in multidisciplinary teams, and contribute to medical advancements. As the medical field evolves, so too will the language we use, requiring all healthcare professionals to adapt and grow in their linguistic competencies.

This exploration into everyday medical terminology sets the stage for deeper studies and practical experiences that will define the careers of healthcare professionals. The next chapters will build on this foundation, focusing on the application of this terminology in specialized medical fields, enhancing both understanding and expertise in the vast world of medicine.

Chapter 7
Practice Makes Perfect
Emphasizing the Importance of Reinforcement in Learning

Chapter 7, "Practice Makes Perfect," recognizes the critical role that consistent practice and reinforcement play in mastering medical terminology. This chapter is dedicated to providing tools and techniques that enhance retention and deepen understanding of the extensive and sometimes complex language used in healthcare. By actively engaging with the material through various methods of reinforcement, learners can solidify their grasp of medical terminology, which is foundational for effective communication and practice in the medical field.

Structured Approach to Reinforcement

In this chapter, we explore structured methods to ensure that the medical terminology learned in previous chapters is not only understood but also retained long-term. These methods are designed to cater to diverse learning styles and preferences, offering multiple pathways to mastery:

- **Practice Questions**: This section will offer a series of practice questions that cover a broad spectrum of medical terminology. These questions are designed to challenge learners and encourage them to apply their knowledge in different contexts, enhancing both recall and understanding.

- **Flashcards**: One of the most effective tools for memorization, flashcards help in the reinforcement of medical terms by promoting active recall. This section provides tips on creating effective flashcards and strategies for using them to maximize learning. Suggestions include organizing flashcards by category, such as body systems or conditions, and incorporating images or diagrams to enhance visual learning.
- **Quizzes**: Periodic quizzes serve as an essential tool for self-assessment and help learners gauge their progress over time. This section will guide how to design quizzes that accurately reflect the depth of knowledge required in medical settings, offering a mix of question types from multiple-choice to short answer formats.

Educational Objectives of Chapter 8

The overarching goal of this chapter is to equip students and healthcare professionals with practical tools to ensure that their learning is not fleeting but instead leaves a lasting impression. By regularly engaging with practice questions, creating and utilizing flashcards, and assessing themselves through quizzes, learners can build a robust vocabulary of medical terms that they can recall swiftly and accurately.

Conclusion and Transition

In conclusion, "Practice Makes Perfect" is more than just a mantra; it is a necessary part of learning medical terminology effectively. As learners progress through this chapter, they will develop a stronger, more intuitive grasp of medical language, preparing them for the practical realities of healthcare environments. The strategies discussed here are not only theoretical but are intended for active and ongoing application, ensuring that learners remain competent and confident in their medical communication skills.

As we move beyond this chapter, learners will be encouraged to continue practicing and revisiting the material, fostering a cycle of continuous learning and improvement essential for any medical professional.

Comprehensive Exploration of Structured Approach to Reinforcement

Mastering medical terminology is not merely about exposure to the words and their meanings; it requires a systematic approach to learning and retaining this extensive vocabulary effectively. Chapter 8 delves into structured reinforcement methods that are tailored to meet the needs of diverse learning styles and preferences, ensuring that learners can retain and apply medical terminology proficiently over the long term.

Practice Questions
Purpose of Practice Questions

Practice questions serve as a vital tool in the educational arsenal of any medical student or healthcare professional. They are designed to consolidate learning by challenging the learner to recall and apply medical terminology in various contexts. The purpose of these questions is multifaceted:

- **Reinforcement of Learning**: Regular interaction with practice questions helps solidify the retention of medical terms, ensuring that learners can recall information accurately when needed.
- **Identification of Weak Areas**: Practice questions help learners identify areas where their understanding may be lacking, allowing them to focus their subsequent study efforts more effectively.

- **Simulation of Real-World Scenarios**: These questions often simulate scenarios that a healthcare professional might encounter, providing a practical context to theoretical knowledge, which enhances deeper understanding and preparation for real-life applications.

Impact of Practice Questions

The impact of incorporating practice questions into medical education is significant:

- **Enhanced Retention**: The process of actively recalling information through practice questions improves long-term retention of medical terminology. This active recall is more effective than passive review techniques such as reading or listening.
- **Improved Test Performance**: Regular practice with these questions prepares students for formal assessments by familiarizing them with the format and types of questions they may encounter, thereby reducing test anxiety and improving performance.
- **Development of Critical Thinking**: By engaging with complex scenarios that require the application of multiple pieces of knowledge, learners develop critical thinking and problem-solving skills that are essential in medical practice.

Application and Examples of Practice Questions

To illustrate the practical application of medical terminology through practice questions, let's consider a few examples across different categories:

1. **Basic Recall**:
2. **Question**: What does the prefix "hypo-" mean in medical terms?

3. **Answer**: "Hypo-" means under, beneath, or less than normal.
4. **Scenario-Based Application**:
5. **Question**: A patient arrives exhibiting signs of 'tachypnea'. What condition is this, and what might it indicate about the patient's health?
6. **Answer**: Tachypnea refers to rapid breathing. It may indicate respiratory distress, an infection, or another condition like metabolic acidosis.
7. **Image-Based Diagnosis**:
8. **Question**: [Image of a skin rash] Identify the type of rash shown and list two potential causes.
9. **Answer**: The image shows a 'maculopapular rash', which could be caused by measles or an allergic drug reaction.
10. **Cross-Specialty Integration**:
11. **Question**: How would you explain the term "cardiomegaly" to a patient, and why might a radiologist be involved in diagnosing this condition?
12. **Answer**: Cardiomegaly means enlargement of the heart. A radiologist might be involved to perform and interpret an X-ray or other imaging studies to confirm this diagnosis and assess its severity.
13. **Treatment Planning**:
14. **Question**: If a patient is diagnosed with 'osteoporosis', what types of medical terms might you encounter in discussing treatment options?
15. **Answer**: Terms might include "bisphosphonates", "calcium supplements", and "DEXA scan" for bone density measurement.
16. **What does the suffix "-ectomy" signify in medical terms?**

- Answer: Removal of a body part, typically by surgery.

1. **Define 'bradycardia' and discuss possible clinical implications.**

   - Answer: Bradycardia is a slower than normal heart rate. It can be benign in athletes or signify a problem like heart block or hypothyroidism.

1. **Explain the term 'hyperglycemia' and its possible health risks.**

   - Answer: Hyperglycemia refers to high blood glucose levels, which if persistent, can lead to complications such as diabetic neuropathy, kidney damage, or cardiovascular disease.

1. **What is 'dysphagia' and what are two common causes?**

   - Answer: Dysphagia is difficulty swallowing and can be caused by neurological disorders like Parkinson's disease or physical obstructions like esophageal cancer.

1. **Identify the term that describes inflammation of the liver.**

   - Answer: Hepatitis.

1. **What does 'idiopathic' mean in a medical context?**

   - Answer: It refers to a disease or condition that has no known cause.

1. **Define 'contraindication' and give an example.**

- Answer: A contraindication is a situation or condition that makes a specific treatment or procedure potentially unsafe. Example: Use of a medication to which a patient is allergic.

1. **What is meant by 'neonatology'?**

- Answer: The branch of medicine that deals with the care, development, and diseases of newborns.

1. **Explain 'renal failure' and two of its potential treatments.**

- Answer: Renal failure is a medical condition in which the kidneys fail to adequately filter waste products from the blood. Treatments can include dialysis or kidney transplantation.

1. **What medical term describes low bone density?**

- Answer: Osteopenia.

1. **Define 'anaphylaxis' and describe its immediate treatment protocol.**

- Answer: Anaphylaxis is a severe, potentially life-threatening allergic reaction. Immediate treatment includes administration of epinephrine and calling emergency medical services.

1. **What does 'psychosomatic' imply when describing a medical condition?**

- Answer: It refers to physical symptoms that are caused or aggravated by mental factors such as internal conflict or stress.

1. **Describe the implications of 'antibiotic resistance'.**

- Answer: Antibiotic resistance occurs when bacteria change in response to the use of these medicines, making the antibiotics less effective and infections harder to treat.

1. **What is 'palliative care'?**

- Answer: A specialized area of healthcare that focuses on relieving and preventing the suffering of patients.

1. **Define 'sphygmomanometer' and its use.**

- Answer: A device used to measure blood pressure.

1. **What is 'menorrhagia' and what are some potential treatment options?**

- Answer: Menorrhagia is excessively heavy menstrual bleeding. Treatments can include hormonal therapy, uterine artery embolization, or surgical options.

1. **Explain 'bilateral salpingo-oophorectomy'.**

- Answer: Surgical removal of both ovaries and fallopian tubes.

1. **What does 'cerebrovascular accident' refer to?**

- Answer: Another term for a stroke, specifically related to an interruption or reduction of blood flow to the brain.

1. **Describe what is measured by 'hemoglobin A1c' tests.**

- Answer: This test measures the average levels of blood glucose over the past three months, used primarily to diagnose and monitor diabetes.

1. **What is 'thrombocytopenia'?**

- Answer: A condition characterized by abnormally low levels of platelets in the blood.

Practice questions are an indispensable part of medical education, offering a robust method to enhance learning, test knowledge, and prepare for real-life medical situations. By integrating these questions into their study routines, learners not only improve their grasp of medical terminology but also prepare themselves for the practical demands of healthcare professions, where accurate knowledge and quick thinking are paramount.

Understanding Design and Implementation

In medical education, practice questions are essential for deepening understanding and enhancing the ability to apply knowledge practically. These questions range from basic definitions to complex clinical scenarios, designed to stimulate critical thinking and practical application. This approach helps integrate various medical concepts, reinforcing learning, identifying areas for improvement, and preparing students for real-world medical situations.

The Role of Well-Designed Questions

Effective practice questions serve multiple educational purposes: they reinforce learning, help identify knowledge gaps, and encourage the integration of different medical concepts. Below, we present a varied set of questions with answers, each designed to engage different aspects of medical learning:

1. **What is the medical term for high blood pressure?**
2. Answer: Hypertension.
3. **Define 'tachycardia'.**
4. Answer: An abnormally fast heart rate.
5. **Explain the difference between 'benign' and 'malignant'.**
6. Answer: Benign refers to a condition that is not harmful in the long term, whereas malignant refers to a severe and progressively worsening disease, often used to describe cancer.
7. **What does 'idiopathic' imply about the cause of a condition?**
8. Answer: Idiopathic means that the condition has no identifiable external cause.
9. **Describe the role of 'antibodies' in the immune system.**
10. Answer: Antibodies are proteins produced by the immune system that detect and neutralize foreign objects like bacteria and viruses.
11. **What is the function of the pancreas in the digestive system?**

12. Answer: The pancreas produces enzymes that help in digestion and hormones like insulin that regulate blood sugar levels.

13. **Identify and describe the function of three major types of blood cells.**

14. Answer: Red blood cells carry oxygen, white blood cells fight infections, and platelets help in blood clotting.

15. **What does the prefix 'hypo-' signify in medical terms like 'hypoglycemia'?**

16. Answer: Hypo- means below normal; hypoglycemia refers to lower than normal blood sugar levels.

17. **Define 'osteoporosis' and discuss potential treatments.**

18. Answer: Osteoporosis is a bone disease characterized by bone weakening, increasing the risk of fractures. Treatments include calcium and vitamin D supplements, and medications like bisphosphonates.

19. **Describe the pathophysiology of asthma.**

20. Answer: Asthma is characterized by chronic inflammation of the airways which leads to episodes of wheezing, breathlessness, chest tightness, and coughing.

21. **What is 'anemia'? Provide three possible causes.**

22. Answer: Anemia is a condition in which there is a deficiency of red blood cells or hemoglobin. Causes include iron deficiency, chronic disease, or bone marrow problems.

23. **Explain the significance of the 'QRS complex' in an ECG reading.**

24. Answer: The QRS complex represents the rapid depolarization of the right and left ventricles, indicating ventricular activity.

25. **What are 'opioids', and what risks are associated with their use?**

26. Answer: Opioids are a class of drugs that act on the nervous system to relieve pain. Risks include dependency, overdose, and death.

27. **Define 'endoscopy' and list two conditions it can help diagnose.**

28. Answer: Endoscopy is a procedure using a scope to view the interior of a body cavity. It can diagnose conditions like stomach ulcers and colorectal cancer.

29. **What is a 'biopsy' and when might it be necessary?**

30. Answer: A biopsy involves removing a small piece of tissue for examination. It's necessary for diagnosing cancers and other diseases.

31. **Describe the term 'autoimmune disease' with two examples.**

32. Answer: Autoimmune diseases occur when the immune system attacks the body's own tissues. Examples include rheumatoid arthritis and type 1 diabetes.

33. **What is meant by 'chronic' in terms of disease duration?**

34. Answer: Chronic refers to a long-duration, persistent disease often with slow progression.

35. **Explain the medical use of the term 'invasive' concerning diagnostic techniques.**

36. Answer: Invasive diagnostic techniques involve entering the body, usually with instruments like scopes or needles, e.g., laparoscopy.

37. **What is 'dialysis' used for?**

38. Answer: Dialysis is a procedure to remove waste products and excess fluid from the blood when the kidneys stop working properly.

39. **Define 'arrhythmia' and provide an example.**

40. Answer: Arrhythmia is an irregular heartbeat. An example is atrial fibrillation.

41. **What is the medical term for a stroke, and what are its primary symptoms?**

42. Answer: The medical term for a stroke is cerebrovascular accident (CVA). Primary symptoms include sudden numbness or weakness in the face, arm, or leg, especially on one side of the body; confusion; trouble speaking; and loss of balance or coordination.

43. **Explain 'congenital' in the context of medical conditions.**

44. Answer: Congenital refers to conditions that are present at birth, whether they are inherited or caused by the environment.

45. **What are 'corticosteroids', and for what conditions are they commonly prescribed?**

46. Answer: Corticosteroids are anti-inflammatory drugs prescribed for conditions like asthma, allergies, and autoimmune diseases.

47. **Describe the difference between 'viral' and 'bacterial' infections.**

48. Answer: Viral infections are caused by viruses and often resolve without treatment, while bacterial infections are caused by bacteria and can often be treated with antibiotics.

49. **What does 'metastasis' mean in the context of cancer?**

50. Answer: Metastasis refers to the spread of cancer cells from the original tumor site to other parts of the body.

Encouraging Regular Practice

Learners should engage with these questions regularly as part of their study routine to enhance both memorization and the ability to rapidly recall and apply complex medical terminology. Regular practice facilitates a deeper understanding of medical terms and their use in various clinical contexts, thus preparing students effectively for their future roles in healthcare environments.

As medical science evolves, so too should the practice questions used in medical education. It's important for learners to continuously challenge themselves with new questions that reflect the latest medical research and clinical practices. Additionally, incorporating feedback into the learning process—whether through self-assessment, peer discussions, or educational software—can significantly enhance understanding and retention of complex medical concepts.

In conclusion, the careful design and regular implementation of practice questions are fundamental in medical education. They not only solidify knowledge but also develop the critical thinking and problem-solving skills essential for medical practice. By regularly challenging themselves with a broad spectrum of questions, learners can ensure they are well-prepared to meet the demands of the healthcare profession and provide the highest quality of care.

Flashcards as a Learning Tool

Flashcards are a quintessential tool in medical education, valued for their simplicity and efficacy in facilitating active recall. This method not only aids in memorizing vast amounts of medical terminology but also significantly enhances long-term retention. This section aims to guide learners through the effective creation and utilization of flashcards, turning a basic memorization tool into a powerful component of their learning strategy.

Designing Effective Flashcards

1. **Content Selection**: The first step in creating flashcards is to select the content judiciously. For medical students, this typically involves key terms, definitions, diagnostic criteria, symptoms, and treatment protocols. Each flashcard should focus on a single concept to avoid cognitive overload.

2. **Visual Enhancements**: Incorporating images, diagrams, or anatomical illustrations can drastically

improve the effectiveness of flashcards. Visual aids help in creating mental images and associations that are easier to recall. For instance, a flashcard for "myocardial infarction" might include a diagram of the heart highlighting areas typically affected by the condition.

3. **Engaging Content**: To make flashcards more engaging, include mnemonics, colorful markers, or even humorous phrases that relate to the medical terms. This not only makes the learning process more enjoyable but also aids in retention.

4. **Categorization**: Organizing flashcards into categories such as body systems (cardiovascular, respiratory), types of diseases (infectious, chronic), or processes (metabolism, homeostasis) helps structure the learning process and makes revision sessions more efficient.

Utilization Strategies for Flashcards

1. **Spaced Repetition**: One of the most effective techniques for using flashcards is spaced repetition. This method involves reviewing flashcards at systematically increasing intervals to reinforce memory. Software and apps designed for spaced repetition can automate this process, scheduling reviews at optimal times to enhance memory retention.

2. **Active Recall Sessions**: Regularly test yourself with your set of flashcards. Active recall promotes deeper learning and helps in identifying weak areas that need further reinforcement. This process is crucial right before exams and as ongoing preparation for practical applications.

3. **Peer Learning**: Engaging with peers in flashcard sessions can introduce a collaborative element to learning. Testing each other with flashcards can provide

new insights and explanations, enriching the learning experience and making it more interactive.

4. **Contextual Application**: Try to apply the terms from your flashcards to clinical scenarios or case studies. This practice helps in understanding not just the definition but also the application of terms in real-life contexts, preparing students for practical, hands-on experiences in their medical training.

Flashcards are more than just a tool for rote memorization; they are a versatile component of effective learning in medical education. By carefully designing, organizing, and utilizing flashcards, medical students can greatly enhance their mastery of complex medical terminology. The strategies outlined here encourage not only individual study but also cooperative learning, making the journey through medical education both effective and enjoyable. As learners progress, continuously updating and revising their flashcard decks to include new information and insights ensures that their knowledge remains current and comprehensive.

Quizzes as a Learning Tool

Quizzes play an indispensable role in medical education, serving as a dynamic self-assessment mechanism that allows learners to measure their understanding and progress. They are not only diagnostic tools but also essential for reinforcing learning, identifying knowledge gaps, and ensuring readiness for professional practice.

Purpose and Benefits of Periodic Quizzes

1. **Continuous Self-Assessment**: Quizzes provide immediate feedback on a learner's understanding of the material, highlighting strengths and pinpointing areas that need improvement. This ongoing self-assessment is crucial for guiding studies and preparation effectively.

2. **Reinforcement of Learning**: The act of recalling information during a quiz enhances memory retention and aids in the transition of knowledge from short-term to long-term memory, a process vital for the rigorous demands of medical professions.

3. **Identification of Gaps**: Regular quizzes help learners identify gaps in their knowledge, allowing them to focus their subsequent study efforts more efficiently and effectively.

Quiz Construction Strategies

1. **Designing Effective Quizzes**: The construction of quizzes requires thoughtful consideration of the content's breadth and depth. This section provides guidelines on creating quizzes that accurately reflect the medical terminology used in professional settings.
2. **Incorporating Various Question Types**:
3. **Multiple-Choice**: These questions are excellent for testing a wide range of knowledge efficiently and are particularly useful for drilling on specifics, such as terminology or symptomatology.
4. **True/False**: Quick and straightforward, these questions are good for reinforcing factual knowledge and clarifying misconceptions.
5. **Fill-in-the-Blank**: Effective for testing the precise recall of medical terms or processes.
6. **Short Answer**: These questions require more detailed responses and are useful for assessing the ability to articulate concepts or processes clearly.
7. **Balancing Difficulty**: The quiz should balance straightforward questions with more challenging ones that require critical thinking or the integration of

multiple pieces of knowledge, mimicking the complexity of real-world medical decision-making.

Implementing Quizzes

1. **Frequency of Quizzes**: Regular quizzes are recommended to keep learners engaged and to continually assess and reinforce learning. The ideal frequency can vary depending on the course structure, but weekly quizzes are common in many educational settings.

2. **Feedback Mechanisms**: Providing detailed explanations for both correct and incorrect answers is crucial for quizzes to be effective learning tools. Timely feedback helps learners understand their mistakes, grasp complex concepts, and avoid repeating errors.

3. **Utilizing Technology**: Digital platforms can be used to administer quizzes, offering automatic scoring and instant feedback. This technology can also track progress over time, providing learners with insights into their learning trends and needs.

Quizzes are more than just tests; they are integral to the educational process, particularly in fields as demanding as medicine. By regularly engaging with well-constructed quizzes, medical students and professionals can ensure a deep and lasting understanding of essential medical terminology and concepts. This proactive approach to learning helps prepare them not only for exams but also for the complex decision-making required in clinical settings. As learners continue to develop their skills and knowledge, quizzes remain a valuable tool for ensuring they are both competent and confident in their professional capabilities.

The structured approaches to reinforcement discussed in Chapter

8 are essential for anyone serious about fully integrating medical terminology into their professional lexicon. By engaging with practice questions, utilizing flashcards, and testing themselves through quizzes, learners not only enhance their immediate recall of terms but also solidify their long-term understanding of the language used in health-care. This chapter empowers learners to take active steps towards mastery, ensuring that they are well-prepared to use medical termi-nology accurately and confidently in any medical context.

Chapter 8, "Practice Makes Perfect," has underscored the pivotal role of continuous practice in mastering medical terminology. Through a diverse range of tools—practice questions, flashcards, and quizzes—this chapter has provided a structured approach to ensure that learners not only acquire but also retain the vast amount of infor-mation required in the medical field. This ongoing practice is crucial for converting theoretical knowledge into practical skills, essential for every healthcare professional.

The practice methods discussed in this chapter help reinforce learning, allowing medical students and professionals to solidify their understanding of complex medical terms and concepts. Regularly engaging with these tools ensures that knowledge becomes second nature, reducing the cognitive load during critical clinical situations where quick and accurate recall is paramount.

Practice questions, as explored, are not merely tools for assess-ment but catalysts for deeper understanding. They challenge learners to apply their knowledge in varied contexts, enhancing both recall and comprehension. This active approach to learning is vital for preparing for real-world applications where medical terminology is used in diagnosing and treating patients.

Flashcards have been highlighted as effective tools for memoriza-tion, particularly useful in mastering the vast array of medical termi-nology. By encouraging active recall and spaced repetition, flashcards help embed information deeply into long-term memory, making recall faster and more intuitive. This method is especially beneficial for visual learners who benefit from the visual aids that can be incorporated into flashcards.

Quizzes serve as critical checkpoints for learners to assess their understanding and track their progress. They provide immediate feedback, helping learners identify areas of strength and those requiring further study. This self-assessment drives improvement and helps maintain a consistent level of competence, which is essential in the ever-evolving field of medicine.

Chapter 8 promotes a culture of continuous learning and improvement, fundamental in the medical profession. The learning strategies presented are designed to be integrated into regular study routines, fostering a habit of lifelong learning. This habit is crucial for medical professionals who must stay abreast of new research, evolving technologies, and emerging health challenges.

As we conclude Chapter 8 and look towards the future, the emphasis remains on the importance of practice in the mastery of medical terminology and beyond. The skills honed through the structured learning and practice methods detailed in this chapter lay the foundation for proficient and confident medical professionals. These practices not only prepare learners for exams but also for their future roles where they will apply this knowledge to real-life medical scenarios, ultimately enhancing patient care and medical outcomes. Moving forward, learners are encouraged to continue using these tools, exploring new ways to integrate practice into their daily learning, and always striving toward excellence in their professional journey.

Conclusion to the Medical Terminology Study Guide

This guide has taken you on an extensive journey through the intricate landscape of medical terminology, offering a structured and comprehensive pathway to mastering the essential terms used across various aspects of the healthcare field. From the foundational building blocks of medical language—such as roots, prefixes, and suffixes—to a more detailed exploration of body systems, diagnostic procedures, and medical specialties, this text has equipped you with the fundamental knowledge crucial for success in healthcare professions.

Each chapter methodically breaks down the major body systems, providing a thorough understanding of the terminology associated with each system's anatomy, functions, and common disorders. This guide also delves into various medical specialties, shedding light on the specific language used by professionals in fields ranging from cardiology to neurology, enhancing both your understanding and your ability to communicate effectively within these domains.

Understanding medical terminology is crucial for effectively diagnosing and treating patients, which is why this guide emphasizes its practical application in modern medicine. Detailed discussions on how medical terms are used in conjunction with today's diagnostic tools—from blood tests to advanced imaging techniques—are included to ensure you can apply this knowledge practically and with confidence.

To aid in the absorption and long-term retention of the covered material, the guide introduces a variety of effective learning tools and strategies. Whether through the use of flashcards to promote active recall or engaging with practice questions and quizzes designed to test and reinforce your understanding, these strategies are tailored to enhance your learning experience and prepare you for both examinations and real-world medical situations.

The guide underscores the importance of not only understanding medical terminology but also applying it effectively in everyday healthcare settings. The ability to accurately interpret medical charts, communicate with colleagues, and explain conditions to patients is crucial and requires a fluent command of medical language. Furthermore, the guide encourages ongoing education and engagement with new medical terminology as medicine evolves, highlighting the necessity of lifelong learning in maintaining proficiency and staying current with medical advancements.

This summary captures the essence of what has been covered throughout this guide, reflecting the depth and breadth of the material presented. Designed to serve as a comprehensive educational tool, this guide aims to not just impart knowledge but to foster a deep understanding and practical application of medical terminology, thus enhancing both your professional growth and the quality of care you provide as a healthcare professional. As you continue your journey in medicine, let this guide be a foundational resource that you can continually refer back to, ensuring your medical terminology skills remain sharp and effective.

Encouragement to Keep Learning

As you continue on your journey in the medical field, remember that learning medical terminology is a continuous process. Medicine is an ever-evolving science, with new terms, treatments, and technologies emerging regularly. Staying updated with medical terminology will enhance your ability to communicate with colleagues, perform your duties effectively, and contribute to better patient outcomes.

Let this guide be a foundation upon which you build a robust medical vocabulary. Approach each new term and concept with curiosity and determination. Engage actively with the material, revisit chapters to reinforce your understanding, and use the practice tools regularly to test your knowledge.

Remember, every medical professional was once a beginner. Your ability to master medical terminology will grow with time and experience. Stay committed to your learning, embrace challenges as opportunities to improve, and continue to expand your knowledge. Your dedication to mastering medical terminology is not just an academic exercise—it's a vital part of your journey to becoming a compassionate and competent healthcare provider.

Stay motivated, remain persistent, and keep pushing the boundaries of your knowledge. The effort you put into learning today will pave the way for your success tomorrow. Embrace the lifelong journey of learning, and let the knowledge you gain empower you to make a positive impact in the world of medicine.

www.ingramcontent.com/pod-product-compliance
Lightning Source LLC
Chambersburg PA
CBHW071643170726
48000CB00023B/210